D0146106

Subtle Suicide

Subtle Suicide

Our Silent Epidemic
of Ambivalence about Living

MICHAEL A. CHURCH AND
CHARLES I. BROOKS

PRAEGER
An Imprint of ABC-CLIO, LLC

A B C CLIO

Santa Barbara, California • Denver, Colorado • Oxford, England

Library of Congress Cataloging-in-Publication Data
Church, Michael A., 1947–
    Subtle suicide : our silent epidemic of ambivalence about living /
Michael A. Church and Charles I. Brooks.
        p. cm.
    Includes bibliographical references and index.
    ISBN 978-0-313-38066-2 (hardcopy : alk. paper) — ISBN 978-0-313-38067-9
(ebook)
    1. Suicide—Psychology. 2. Self-destructive behavior. 3. Uncertainty.
4. Suicide—Case studies. I. Brooks, Charles I., 1944– II. Title.
RC569.C487 2009
362.28—dc22   2009016661

13   12   11   10   09   1   2   3   4   5

This book is also available on the World Wide Web as an eBook.
Visit www.abc-clio.com for details.

ABC-CLIO, LLC
130 Cremona Drive, P.O. Box 1911
Santa Barbara, California 93116-1911

This book is printed on acid-free paper ∞

Manufactured in the United States of America

To our daughters, Dominique, Alondra, Natasha, Audra, and Kelly

Contents

Preface

We have divided this book into two parts. In the first part, we introduce and define the concept of subtle suicide. At its simplest level, "subtle suicide" describes the dynamics of people who, though they may not overtly and genuinely try to kill themselves, nevertheless lead self-destructive lives because they honestly do not care if they live or die. Throughout our discussion, we use real case studies from our files to illustrate the variety of subtle suicide actions and some of the family dynamics that seem to reappear over many different cases. We end Part I with a chapter on how family members can identify and help the subtle suicide victim. This chapter is a practical, hands-on discussion to answer questions like, "What do I do and what do I say when I suspect someone I care for is moving down the subtle suicide road?"

Part II is written more for the college undergraduate or graduate student and for professionals who work with clients in a counseling context. Here, we provide some historical context for the notion of subtle suicide and touch a bit on theoretical distinctions between our concept and similar ones offered by previous theorists and researchers. We end the second part with a discussion of the need for a formal instrument to measure subtle suicide and distinguish it from other diagnostic conditions.

Recognition of subtle suicide behavior is hardly new in psychology, but our treatment of it is. We stress how subtle suicide is often misdiagnosed as bipolar disorder or any one of a number of other psychological disorders, or as an addiction like gambling or alcohol/drug abuse. In the case of subtle suicide, such addictions are symptoms of deeper psychological conflicts. We have found that when people suffering from subtle suicide are made aware of their condition, they no longer feel alone and isolated. Furthermore, any addictive behaviors they are showing begin to make sense to them as symptoms of a deeper problem. By the same token, they realize that diagnoses stressing depression or anxiety as their fundamental problem are misplaced, and they understand why psychiatric medications so often fail to bring them any long-term relief. In this book, we also note that when family members and professionals reach these same understandings and insights, both the sufferer and significant others can be "on the same page" and work together to defeat this silent enemy.

We would like to thank our wives, Nelya and Joyce, for their emotional support. In addition, we thank Melanie Bradshaw, Kristy Cerullo, Jennifer Derby, Heidi Pierson, and Amilynn Savner for their contributions and help in preparation of the manuscript.

Introduction

We all know people who are living "on the edge" and, at the same time, wasting their lives. Some of these people we know quite well, and others only at a distance. One way or another, we have become aware of their risky behaviors, self-neglect, carelessness, and negative mood states. Sometimes we hear them express pessimistic and depressive thoughts and beliefs. In these persons, we observe a huge waste of human potential. Worse, even tragically, we see people who become sick more frequently than most, and who may die prematurely or suddenly as a result of their self-defeating actions.

We all have felt the helplessness associated with witnessing these types of individuals, people who seem to adopt a "who cares?" attitude about themselves and life. The distinguishing characteristic of these people is ambivalence: "I could care less if I live or die."

This book is written for all who have experienced, directly or indirectly, these sorts of behaviors, perceptions, and feelings. It is our hope that both those who have suffered or are suffering from this kind of lifestyle and those who attempt to help them will find the concepts in this book both illuminating and helpful in dealing with this all-too-common life pattern that we call *subtle suicide*.

We write this book for four reasons. First, we want to make readers more aware of the concept of subtle suicide and how many millions of people suffer from the condition. We are confident you will find this concept relevant because you have at least one friend, relative, or acquaintance who suffers from this condition.

Second, we want to cover the causes of subtle suicide. This analysis allows us to suggest some preventive measures, as well as to discuss strategies for treating this condition earlier and more effectively.

Third, we want to review the negative impact of subtle suicide, on both sufferers and their significant others. Having knowledge of these effects can potentially motivate both the victims and those around them to avoid or minimize the detrimental and demoralizing consequences of this condition.

Finally, we want to discuss strategies to combat this devastating problem. No one is born with a desire to become a self-defeating and self-destructive person and suffer an unnecessary loss of positive life experiences. Yet, too many people in our society find themselves in this situation. We believe there are many methods available to treat such a problem. Unfortunately, both the subtle suicide condition and the methods available to treat it are too often neglected in the mental health profession. We want to correct this oversight.

Senior author Michael Church became interested in the notion of subtle suicide years ago after he heard many outpatient clients essentially saying that they were "sort of" suicidal. They did not actually use the term *subtle,* but the underlying nature of their thinking was implied by statements like:

- "Don't worry that I'll try and commit suicide. After all, I don't want to be committed to the psych ward. But almost every night I feel that if I don't wake up tomorrow, then that's okay."
- "I'm not going to deliberately try to kill myself, but if I stepped off a curb and a bus ran over me, that would be okay."
- "I don't want to hurt myself and others by committing suicide, but I plan to continue smoking heavily so I can die sooner of lung cancer or other problems."

As Church saw these and similar ideas expressed in his group therapy sessions with psychiatric clients, he became convinced of the need for an analysis of this subtle process of self-destruction. Working with this type of client on a regular basis focused his thinking, and he continued his collaboration with Charles Brooks, his coauthor of an earlier work (*How Psychology Applies to Everyday Life,* Greenwood Press, 2009). Both of us believe a book analyzing subtle suicide is long overdue and can help lay readers, students, and professionals to think differently about people who are subtly suicidal and to understand better the dynamics of this condition.

Extensive experience in performing individual and group therapy allowed Church to see the underlying processes of subtle suicide at work in many people. The case studies of clients in therapy described in this book to illustrate different aspects of subtle suicide are from his practice. Not all of our case examples, however, involve outpatient or hospitalized clients. We also draw upon our experiences with colleagues, students, acquaintances, and relatives. We found it relatively easy to identify many people who fit the profile. That is why we believe subtle suicide is a condition of epidemic proportions. Unfortunately, because the condition is often misdiagnosed, we also see it as a *silent* epidemic. We are quite sure, however, that after reading this book, you will also be able to identify many people who are suffering from this dangerous condition and become aware of steps you can take to help them.

We have taken considerable care to protect the identities of persons discussed in this book. We often change gender, age, status, ethnicity, or other aspects of the case, without modifying its underlying dynamics. In fact, we can say confidently that if you are one of Michael Church's clients or have contact with either of us at any level (student, friend, relative, etc.) and think you recognize yourself in this book, you are probably wrong.

_____ *Part I* _____

The Basics of Subtle Suicide

Chapter 1

Defining Subtle Suicide

JACK

Let's begin our journey into the world of subtle suicide with the case of Jack, a man who, from childhood into adulthood, consistently avoided negative emotions and responsibility for his actions. The older of two children, Jack came from a working-class family. He was always a physically large, overweight boy, and the other kids typically made fun of him. Consequently, he never developed much self-confidence and had pretty low self-esteem.

Jack's family never had a lot of money. His home life during his childhood cannot be described as overflowing with warmth and love. In fact, the primary source of acceptance, praise, and "love" in Jack's family seemed to be food. There was always lots to eat, and the parents rewarded their kids for "eating well," which really meant overeating. Whenever the kids came home from school, Mom was in the kitchen cooking, ready to welcome them with all sorts of treats. Jack's father, on the other hand, was a domineering, cold, and harsh parent. In fact, other kids and their parents who knew him called him "Khrushchev," after the prime minister of the Soviet Union when Jack was a young boy. We do not know if Jack's father physically abused him; when his wife asked him about this possibility, Jack refused to give a direct answer.

In high school and college, Jack was not overly popular, but he did have a small group of peers to hang out with. For the most part, these were quiet years, as Jack got acceptable grades and stayed below the radar, so to speak. He plugged along, avoiding challenge and confrontation. He quietly did his work and kept out of trouble.

After graduation from college, Jack got a job, met a girl, got married, and began a family. Unfortunately, he continued to avoid facing the increasing challenges of life. Jack's wife, Brenda, ran the household and made most of the decisions, both domestic and financial. When children came along, Brenda became the disciplinarian and primary caretaker. Jack pretty much stayed in the background when it came to guiding and raising his kids, although it was clear he loved the kids.

In his early work years, Jack's employment record was spotty. He was unsuccessful in a couple of jobs and had a failed business venture, but he eventually found a job that gave him some success and financial security. In spite of this success, however, over the years his drinking increased significantly. He spent long hours away from home socializing and drinking while Brenda was home managing the kids and the home. When she confronted him about his need to take on more responsibility and get more involved, he reacted with angry outbursts and refused to discuss the situation. Many friends and work colleagues saw these same patterns of behavior. As Brenda recalls it, Jack worked at all costs to avoid stress or confrontation with her or with anyone else; he would simply "bottle up" his feelings and retreat into silence or even leave the house and go to the local bar. Jack had become what psychologists call an "avoidant personality."

Jack developed some health problems in his early forties, but he kept his symptoms to himself. He chose not to tell Brenda about his pains and not to get checked out by his physician. Once again, he avoided taking action, even though doing so could potentially threaten his very survival. Eventually, however, his cancerous condition became obvious because he developed open, bleeding sores on his skin, and he needed Brenda's help in caring for them. Brenda pleaded with him to go to the doctor, but he stubbornly refused, even as his condition worsened over several years. His denial and avoidant tendencies had by now reached irrational levels. Brenda took extreme action and had him involuntarily committed to a medical facility for diagnosis and treatment. Her actions, unfortunately, came too late. The physicians said his cancer was too advanced and he had only months to live, a prediction that came true within a few weeks, when Jack died.

Jack's story comes to us from personal observations and from Brenda, who struggled mightily, both financially and psychologically, following Jack's death. Looking back at Jack's last years, Brenda says he showed very little compassion for himself or his family. He had become self-preoccupied and disconnected from other people and basically had no sense of purpose or life goals. He did not care about his own life and took no steps to help himself in spite of pleas from Brenda, friends, and colleagues. Nothing seemed to matter to him except avoiding stress at all costs. He avoided basic responsibilities and negative emotions, especially ones that could produce confrontation with others. Jack's lifetime of avoidance had led him into a black hole. And to top it all off, he didn't give a damn!

Jack's behavior had dire effects on others, especially his family. Brenda was left with little money and a mountain of bills. Since Jack's death, she has struggled to support her kids and to come to grips with her own psychological issues. For the most part, she has been successful in both areas, although the personal challenges have been complicated greatly because one of her boys developed Jack's avoidant patterns, which led to serious consequences. Brenda herself has been psychiatrically hospitalized, but both inpatient and outpatient counseling has helped, and her future prognosis is quite good.

INTRODUCING SUBTLE SUICIDE

Jack's case illustrates many of the themes we will develop in this book as we analyze a distinctive behavior pattern we call *subtle suicide*. First of all, note that Jack's life was devoted to avoidance of any sort of conflict. However, such a strategy is doomed to fail, because life involves conflict and pain, and continuous efforts to avoid them cannot succeed in the long run if one is to thrive. Confronting and dealing with negative emotions and psychological pain are necessary steps if we are to become psychologically strong and healthy. Jack, however, refused to do so. He was overly sensitive to rejection, criticism, embarrassment, and disapproval. Consequently, he chose to avoid conflict that could put him at risk for such outcomes. Unfortunately, when we avoid conflict, our difficulties grow stronger and become more complex, eventually taking us in a downward spiral from which it becomes difficult to escape. Jack never did escape. He became a member of what we call the "living dead."

A second theme in Jack's case is the effect subtle suicide actions have on family members and friends. They often get "sucked into" the black hole of avoidance and find themselves equally trapped. In this book, we will explore the dynamics of subtle suicide from the perspective of others and describe how they can resist being taken down by the victim.

A third theme in Jack's case concerns helping the victim. Through no fault of her own (remember, Jack had gone to extreme lengths to hide his symptoms for a long period of time), Brenda's efforts to intervene on Jack's behalf came too late. But anyone now reading this case and thinking that it reminds them of a loved one who may be going down the same road as Jack would do well to ask: "What can I do? Can I help? What steps can I take to insure that the outcome is different than for Jack?" We will attempt to answer these questions.

Take a minute to think about a person or people you know who are in trouble. What do we mean by "trouble"? Perhaps they have an eating disorder such as anorexia or bulimia. Maybe they are excessive smokers or drinkers or engage in risky sex. The people you're thinking of may be extreme risk takers who drive recklessly, racing down the interstate at 100 mph. Whatever the specifics, by "trouble" we mean those who seem to take a "spit-in-your-face" approach to life, those who always seems to "push the envelope" or tempt fate. You might describe them as "their own worst enemy," "an accident waiting to happen," or as someone who just doesn't fit the "family profile." They are careless and neglectful, or seem to thrive on risky, dangerous, daredevil-like behaviors. They may receive some social praise for their crazy behavior, but underneath it all, you know they are on the edge. *You* sense their vulnerability to disability or death, but *they* seem blind to the dangers they present to themselves—or simply don't care.

These are the types of individuals we will study in this book. You may be one of them! If not, you are likely to know a few of them. Such self-destructive behavior patterns are actually quite common. When these behaviors become part of a *stable* and *ongoing* pattern, they are what we call subtle suicide.

We choose the word *subtle* because these actions are not blatant like what one normally associates with suicide—things like a gunshot to the head or a jump from a bridge. People who fit our subtle suicide profile follow a more insidious, gradual, and steady descent into self-annihilation. We will analyze this process in this book and try to capture the dynamics of what we believe is a silent epidemic of subtle suicide. We will also develop the message that the process can be stopped, or at least minimized, given appropriate knowledge and intervention.

Subtle suicide is more than a list of acts of self-destructiveness. The term refers to a long-term pattern of self-abuse and neglect that can be identified and treated successfully. The subtle suicide profile is not associated with a single, brief act. It is somewhat independent of other existing psychological disorders. That is, subtle suicide may or may not exist alongside depression, anxiety, drug and alcohol abuse/dependency, and other disorders. There are some very depressed, anxious, and even psychotic people who do *not* show characteristics of subtle suicide. The condition, however, often does coexist with antisocial tendencies, a borderline personality, bipolar disorder, and other conditions. This fact can make subtle suicide difficult to recognize and treat.

Let's illustrate what we mean by subtle suicide with some examples:

- A diabetic man stops taking all medications, including psychiatric ones (such as antidepressants or anti-anxiety agents) and his insulin, and shows signs of social withdrawal.
- A teenage girl cuts her wrists repeatedly and suffers from a serious eating disorder and major depression.
- A young man is "accident prone," particularly when riding his motorcycle, sometimes over 120 mph, and has difficulty maintaining a job.
- A woman uses drugs and alcohol habitually and engages in unprotected sex with men she doesn't know.
- A man gambles repeatedly and excessively and is in significant debt. He owes family and friends large sums of money, continually "hits" them for loans, and

is well on the way to losing his family and home. He alienates others with his self-defeating behavior patterns and is developing increasingly stronger symptoms of anxiety and depression.

- A woman has been psychiatrically hospitalized many times with depression. She has a history of sexual abuse and low self-esteem and shows many types of self-destructive behavior.

At first glance, these diverse examples may not appear to have much in common because the "content" of each situation varies considerably. But *are* there common factors? Is there a related theme in each of these examples? Do all these people share some underlying psychological dynamics that drive their negative feelings, thoughts, and behaviors? We believe they can all be instances of subtle suicide.

THE DEFINITION OF SUBTLE SUICIDE

We define subtle suicide as *a pattern of self-destructive feelings, thoughts, and behaviors that take place over a substantial period of time and significantly reduce the quality and possibly the length of one's life.* Note that we separate the effects on quality and length of life. Suicidal behavior is typically thought of as something that shortens life by ending it. Subtle suicide, on the other hand, is self-destructive, but may not end or even shorten one's life. People with a behavior profile of subtle suicide inevitably decrease the quality of their lives, but they may die of natural or other causes long before subtle suicidal processes would have led to their demise. There is nevertheless a substantial loss of quality of life for subtle suicide sufferers. They become the living dead.

The separation of *length* and *quality* is really quite essential to understanding the concept of subtle suicide. When most of us hear the word *suicide*, we immediately think of a life-ending action. And in the discipline of psychology and all the health professions, the study of suicide emphasizes the importance of keeping people alive. When thinking about subtle suicide patterns, however, we need to shift to an emphasis on maximizing the *quality* of life.

CHARACTERISTICS OF SUBTLE SUICIDE

There are several key criteria that define subtle suicide. These include:

- *Patterns of behavior.* Subtle suicide rarely involves a single behavior such as smoking cigarettes, failure to go to the doctor on a regular basis, drinking alcohol, self-abuse, or gambling. These actions, self-defeating as they may be, are best viewed as negative habits when not part of the larger pattern of self-destruction. Remember, subtle suicide is a *pattern of behavior that is self-defeating and self-destructive.* Yes, any of the above individual behaviors may be involved in the pattern, but none of the behaviors alone qualifies someone as fitting the subtle suicide profile.

- *Conscious or unconscious patterns.* In the early stages, we may or may not be aware that our behavior fits a pattern of subtle suicide. In other words, we may or may not realize that a part of us wishes to self-destruct. Much depends on factors like how insightful we are, whether we have received professional counseling, how many brushes with death we have had, and how often our self-destructiveness has actually hurt ourselves or others. Some people show partial awareness of their self-defeating leanings, and it is not difficult for them to acknowledge their self-destructive patterns. Others are surprised by the revelation that there is a strong part of them that would be relieved if they died, and that their behavior patterns illustrate this tendency. Still others are very aware of their self-destructive tendencies.

- *Intense ambivalence.* Subtle suicide involves intense ambivalence about living. The person experiencing this type of internal conflict desperately wants to live, yet simultaneously does *not* want to continue living. There is a strong desire to avoid the painful experiences associated with living and sometimes even to hurt oneself.

- *Time and duration of onset.* Many people experience feelings and behaviors related to subtle suicide in childhood. Children can develop serious eating disorders, try to burn down their house, slip into deep withdrawal and depression, and even make overt attempts at suicide. Adults who become chronic pain patients resulting from accidents or illness can become subtly suicidal within a relatively brief period of time. The elderly can develop these patterns when faced with widowhood, disability, financial strains, or any of a host of conditions associated with growing old. In short, anyone at any age is vulnerable to suffering from subtle suicide, and the onset can be gradual or sudden.

- *No one cause.* The causes of subtle suicide are many and come from a variety of sources, including personal loss through death or disability of loved ones, personal conflicts particular to reaching a significant age, traumatic events, emotional neglect, genetic predispositions for severe psychiatric problems, and experiences that leave the person feeling guilty and shameful. Virtually any overwhelming or threatening life experience can be a potential cause.

- *Variable course.* Depending on a variety of factors and the resources we have, there are many possible outcomes of subtle suicide. Some people linger with this condition for many years until they die from it or other causes. Others deteriorate until they reach the point of overt suicide. Some eventually conquer the affliction. The course of the condition depends on factors such as quality of support systems, genetic constitution, luck (or lack thereof), and professional intervention.

- *Long-term patterns.* Subtle suicide needs to be distinguished from the relatively brief reactions to some form of acute stress or loss—divorce, death of a loved one, loss of a job, and so on. Subtle suicide becomes a way of life over an extended period of time. Affected individuals stop caring about their life in many important ways and reduce their quality (and sometimes length) of life.

- *Self-defeating spiral.* Subtle desires to die and avoid pain can be great enough to allow habits like carelessness, inattention to personal care, and self-destructive acts become a way of life. Such behavior patterns do not promote health or happiness; in fact, they compromise health and happiness by making life more stressful and difficult. Eventually, the patterns of self-defeat become habitual and chronic, and the victim continues to spiral downward.

- *Condition not readily apparent to others.* People with subtle suicide may be deceptive in their self-defeating patterns and not be open with others about how they actually feel about living. Superficially, they may seem quite normal, especially to acquaintances or casual observers. As a result, individuals who, for instance, cut themselves may be viewed as people who simply are crying out for attention or help, whereas the underlying problems may be much deeper and more serious than others realize.

- *Effects may be delayed for a long time.* The life habits of subtle suicide sufferers can take many years or even decades to catch up with them. Abusing their bodies with drugs or alcohol, eating disorders, self-mutilation, or not taking prescription medication properly ultimately catches up with them. Likewise, failure to act appropriately—things like driving safely, getting regular medical check-ups, exercising, and eating properly—is another path to self-destruction. On the other hand, some forms of subtle suicide can lead to a rather quick downhill slide. For example, diabetics who do not take their insulin, or hypertensives who do not take their blood pressure medication, can quickly get in trouble.

- *Intense negative feelings and thoughts.* Inevitably, subtle suicide sufferers possess a host of negative thoughts and feelings. Typically, they are insecure people who suffer from low self-esteem. They are also pessimistic individuals who feel hopeless about their lives much of the time. Other common characteristics include intense shame and/or guilt, an inability to cope with anger and forgiveness, high degrees of depression and/or anxiety, and a lack of purpose in life.

- *Alienation of others.* Invariably subtle suicide victims alienate family, friends, coworkers, and even health care professionals with their exasperating array of self-defeating behaviors. Although not usually intentional, they frustrate others with their lack of motivation to improve and their self-destructiveness.

As we analyze the dynamics of the subtle suicide profile, we will make the case that subtle suicide is a process worthy of study in its own right, and one that has been largely neglected by the helping professions and behavioral sciences. Historically, the emphasis in research and theorizing about suicide has been on overt suicide. To a certain degree, this focus is understandable. According to 2003 National Youth Violence Prevention Resource Center statistics, suicide is the third leading cause of death in fourteen- to twenty-four-year-olds and the seventh leading cause among five- to fourteen-year-olds. There is little doubt that suicide creates tragic circumstances for those who survive the perpetrator. Nevertheless, we believe that subtle suicide, a more passive and difficult behavior pattern to recognize, occurs more frequently and, in some cases, can even lead to overt suicide. We believe it is time to turn our attention to this all-too-frequent quiet killer that robs so many of both years and quality of life.

IS SUBTLE SUICIDE PATHOLOGICAL?

You may be worried that you or someone you know quite well seems to fit the subtle suicide profile. You resist the idea, however, because you do not want to brand yourself or the other person as "crazy," "abnormal," or "pathological." Such labels can be devastating and can prevent people from seeking help for a genuine psychological problem. We believe that you should put this concern behind you, though, because we do not feel subtle suicide is a true pathological condition that makes the victim "crazy" or "abnormal." Let's look a little deeper into this issue.

Life is not an easy proposition. We develop slowly and are dependent on our caretakers for a very long time. If we are lucky, our parents are pretty stable and not too dysfunctional. In a more or less ideal family situation, our parents are generally loving, supportive, and encouraging. If not, we are relatively powerless to do much to change the situation until we are old enough to become aware that many of our characteristic ways of thinking and acting are self-defeating and destructive. By then, unfortunately, many of our thoughts and actions probably have become habitual. Whatever the case, life challenges us with uncertainties, responsibilities, duties, and losses. Of course, along the way we experience certain degrees of pleasure, typically of short duration, which help balance against the frustrations and pains of our existence. Often, life seems like a ride at Disneyland: we wait forty minutes for two minutes of pleasure.

We like to say that life is usually a 60/40 or 70/30 proposition, in terms of positive and negative events. That is, most of our experiences—say, 60 or 70 percent—we would describe as pleasing and fulfilling, while various stresses, conflicts, and disappointments make up the remainder of our lives. But think about the person who experiences life as 40/60, or worse, on a continuing basis. No one wants to have the bad times consistently outweigh the good times. Doesn't it seem natural (not abnormal) for this person to be ambivalent about life?

From this perspective, it seems to us that subtle suicide can be a natural response to one's life situation. For example, personal care home workers tell us that many elderly residents with no previous psychiatric history show subtle suicide behavior. Thus, whereas subtle suicide can coexist with, and may have causes similar to, a true psychological disorder, subtle suicide is not always a part of some psychological disorder. It may simply represent a response to a very low quality of life.

Subtle suicide victims tend to get caught in a vicious circle that takes them spiraling downward. Certainly they experience negative emotions such as loneliness, depression, and anxiety in large doses. Are these emotions causes of subtle suicide, or are they effects of the condition? We think they can be both. The same can be said about behaviors such as drug abuse, eating disorders, and gambling, which can be either causes or effects of subtle suicide states. One can make the argument that, once the subtle suicide process is in gear, causes may become effects and vice versa. This complexity, of course, makes understanding and treating subtle suicide difficult. To avoid these problems, we think it best to focus primarily on what we see as the root causes of subtle suicide, and we will do so in this book. In our opinion, this is the most fruitful approach with respect to both prevention and treatment efforts, even though some would argue that it is somewhat of an oversimplification. Ultimately, we cannot completely ignore the reality of multiple causations and effects. However, for the victim, the family member, or the friend, developing some basic understanding of the root causes of subtle suicide puts every-one in a better position to understand the condition and produce positive change in the sufferer.

Although we say subtle suicide is not necessarily a pure psychological disorder, the process is certainly related to other disorders. For instance, like other psychological problems, the development of subtle suicide is influenced by four important factors: *risks, vulnerabilities, potentiators,* and *protectors*. We believe it is useful to understand the condition in terms of these well-defined factors, and when we do so, we discover that subtle suicide tendencies typically have their roots early in one's life.

- *Risks.* A risk is any condition that increases the likelihood that psychological problems will develop. Although there is no agreed-upon set of risk factors, some of the more common ones include genetic disorders, low intelligence, physical or emotional abuse, neglect of basic physical or emotional needs, or insecure attachment to a caregiver.

- *Vulnerabilities.* The presence of risk factors increases the likelihood that a child will suffer psychologically. The fact is, however, that some children are more vulnerable to these risks than others. Not all children respond negatively to pov-erty, emotional deprivation, and family conflicts; many, in fact, rise above these risks and go on to productive and successful lives as adults. If, however, a child has vulnerabilities such as a difficult temperament, physical abnormalities or deformities, or poor social skills, that child is more likely to be negatively impacted by the risk factors noted above. Thus, when considering how a child or young adult might begin traveling down a road toward subtle suicide, we must not only look at the person's environmental circumstances but also at their basic personality traits.

- *Potentiators.* These factors complement, strengthen, and magnify the impact of risks. One example is the social isolation that comes from living in a rural area or in a cold, hostile neighborhood. A child who lives in an abusive home might be unable to gain relief from the negative effects of this home life because the neighborhood and general social environment are also abusive. The social envi-ronment, therefore, can add to home-related difficulties.

- *Protectors.* Some factors can counteract the influence of risk factors and help children make positive adjustments despite experiencing risks. Examples include learning tolerance for the views of others and appreciating cultural diversity, having high intelligence, feeling confident and competent, being physically attractive, having good social skills, and experiencing positive adult mentors.

PSYCHOLOGY AND MEDICINE

As psychologists, our book is decidedly oriented toward subtle suicide as it relates to psychological problems. It is important to note, however, that many subtle suicide sufferers make decisions that involve direct threats to their physical welfare. Victims often do things that ravage their bodies and greatly reduce their health. Many cases of subtle suicide occur in a medical context, and physicians, nurses, and other medical specialists are all aware of relevant examples—people who intentionally do not take their prescribed medication, fail to meet scheduled appointments, do not follow up with physical tests, neglect their personal hygiene, and even injure themselves. Self-neglect in diabetic patients has been shown to lead to significant and predictable problems in the circulation system, amputation, and other medical complications or even death. Psychologists have observed significant patterns of self-neglect among chronically ill patients and have found that self-neglect among elderly, clinically ill patients significantly distinguished which patients would be alive a year later. For example, incidents of noncompliance for kidney disease patients on hemodialysis occurred in about 45 percent of the cases. The American death rate due to self-neglect is about four hundred times greater for patients diagnosed with a significant medical problem than for the general population.

Medical conditions can definitely make subtle suicide tendencies much worse. In chapter 3, we will describe cases where medical complications enter the picture and greatly complicate dealing with subtle suicide conditions. The subtle suicide spectrum, therefore, is broad and often crosses over into medical areas. These cases also raise difficult ethical questions, because we are dealing with people who voluntarily choose to interfere with efforts to treat physical conditions. Thus, when we deal with subtle suicide actions, we need to balance patients' rights of autonomy and choice with our responsibility to protect them from self-harm.

We should also not overlook examples of subtle suicide that often result in death, although not directly at the hand of the sufferer. For instance, we know little about people who complete their subtle suicide life patterns by committing "suicide by cop," seeking a doctor-assisted death, or asking for the death penalty while in prison for life. Recently, we had contact with a man who had committed murder. He told his lawyer he wanted the death penalty, not life in prison. He believed his pathetic life was not worth living, but he couldn't imagine killing himself. He wanted the state to do it for him.

There are many things that can get people into these types of subtle suicide areas. Although the case studies we present in this book do not generally touch on sensationalized methods (such as suicide by cop), we believe the dynamics of these cases are basically the same as those cases we do cover. Whatever the individual case and circumstances, we need to understand better these kinds of dynamics and how we can better help these sufferers in the earliest stages of their subtle suicide process, before the subtle suicide train is going at full speed.

DEPTH OF THE PROBLEM

According to statistics, many Americans indulge in self-destructive thinking and behavior:

- More than five million Americans suffer from an eating disorder.
- About 2 percent of our population suffers from pathological gambling, affecting about three to four million adults.
- Only about 10 percent of our population is responsible for 50 percent of the alcohol consumed in our society.
- The lifetime prevalence rate (the proportion of people who develop a certain type of condition at some point during their lifetime) for drug abuse/dependence (nonalcohol) is estimated to be more than 6 percent, and the rate for alcohol dependence is about 13 percent.
- Approximately 20 percent of college students have experienced suicidal thoughts during their college years.
- The lifetime prevalence of severe depression ranges from 10 to 25 percent for women and 5 to 12 percent for men.

Some other relevant statistics:

- A recent Gallup poll showed that 8 to 9 percent of teenagers admitted to engaging in self-destructive acts.
- Self-destructive and suicidal behaviors are relatively common among antisocial and borderline personality clients, who represent about 2 percent of our adult population in each case (about three to four million people each).
- Millions of Americans smoke cigarettes, even though about 87 percent of lung cancer is linked to smoking and it is estimated that each cigarette consumed takes seven minutes off the smoker's life.

This partial list of potentially self-destructive characteristics is testimony to the high percentage of individuals in our society who act in significantly self-defeating and destructive ways. Obviously, there are many other ways a person can show tendencies toward subtle suicide. We are all aware of the alarmingly high rates of self-mutilation (e.g., cutting), especially among adolescents. Moreover, most of us know someone who is an "accident waiting to happen." This is not to say that every person who "cuts" or does risky things is demonstrating evidence of subtle suicide. We need to see more than a single act or behavior pattern to make that judgment. For some, cutting may simply represent a plea for help or attention; for others, it may be an act of conformity or a temporary reaction to stress. As we stressed earlier, to show subtle suicide tendencies, one must show a *stable, habitual pattern* of behavior that is self-destructive or potentially so.

_____ *Chapter 2* _____

Entering the Subtle Suicide Zone

One of our former students, Tom, showed eating behavior that, on the surface, could be interpreted as reflecting subtle suicide. He graduated from college weighing about 440 pounds. Ten years later, at age thirty-one, he tipped the scales at 525. Two things happened that made Tom come to grips with his weight problem. First, he was hospitalized with a variety of physical problems, including high blood pressure, cholesterol, triglyceride, and blood sugar levels, plus blood clots in his legs. The physicians told him that all these problems were because of his weight. Second, in addition to his physical ailments, his mother experienced medical problems and had to be hospitalized briefly.

Suddenly, Tom realized that his weight could indirectly hurt his mother. He faced the fact that he might be unable to help her get through her sickness. For one thing, he had his own physical problems and might even die at a young age. In addition, he was so limited by excessive weight that there would be little he could do to support her in her time of need. After all, he couldn't even tie his own shoelaces! Tom's mother's welfare meant a great deal to him, so he decided to lose a significant amount of weight.

The primary motivation for Tom to change his eating behavior was concern for someone else. "I was basically comfortable with who I was," he recalls. "Sure I was fat, but I was enjoying my life and I had a good circle of friends. But suddenly it hit me—I can't take care of Mom in this condition. How can I take care of her if I'm sick, or if I can't do some basic physical things?" It was also clear to Tom that his life expectancy was low, and he worried, "How can I care for Mom if I die?" His concern for his mother was sincere and genuine. He truly came to see his weight problem as a symbol of selfish indulgence that was a threat to her welfare.

He had to place her well-being first and foremost in his mind. For the first time in his life, Tom had true motivation to take control of his life.

Initially, he thought his only option was stomach surgery. In fact, every professional he talked to—physicians, psychiatrists, and psychologists—tried to convince him that he would never be able to lose sufficient weight on his own; he needed gastric bypass surgery. Tom decided to challenge these opinions, however, and search for alternatives. He first educated himself about nutrition, basic body biology, and exercise through various Web sites on the Internet. He slowly designed a diet for himself that was healthy but limited in calories. He also designed exercise routines, corresponding to movements he could make within the limits imposed by his size. He empowered himself, exercised control over what he alone could change, and took ownership of his diet and exercise plans.

Tom knew his task would be hard to endure and carry out. He realized he would be hungry much of the time and would be tempted to cheat on his diet and exercise program. He also realized he would experience a lot of frustration, but he accepted the fact that he could not control these consequences. "So be it," he thought. "I'll be hungry, tempted to cheat, and frustrated because the whole thing will take time. But I will do it, because it's the only way I can take charge and be there for Mom."

Tom accepted that he was the only person who could change his eating behavior and weight. He stripped away all the excuses for his weight problem: he would not blame genetics, even though his mother was severely overweight; he would not blame McDonald's for supersizing his order of fries and loading them with fats. No, he would challenge these thoughts and not use them to comfort him. Rather, Tom centered his thoughts on one unavoidable truth: his choices—not genetics and not McDonald's—were making him fat. He wisely distinguished between rational and irrational thoughts, both of which he could control.

Within three years, Tom had shed 305 pounds. He still maintains a healthy weight and regular exercise regimen, and now tests at the low end of the scale for cholesterol and triglycerides and has a resting heart rate of 55 (it was nearly 100 when he weighed 525). His mother is now deceased, but he has three new motivators to stay healthy—a wife and two boys.

If we look at Tom when he was in his teens and twenties, we would probably say he fit the category of subtle suicide. His eating behavior was obviously self-destructive, and it appeared he didn't care if he died at a young age. But on closer analysis, this young man was not driven by some desire, unconscious or conscious, to harm himself. In fact, he was thoroughly enjoying his life. He had a good, solid circle of friends, was popular, and did well in school. But while many of his friends spent their leisure time playing video games, Tom occupied himself with eating. He simply liked food and let himself drift into a habitual state of overeating. Only when his mother experienced significant health problems and he became concerned he could not help her because of his extreme obesity did his personal goals change. He took a hard and rational look at the harm he was doing to himself (and indirectly to his mother) and became motivated to get to a physically healthier state.

We share this case to make the point that subtle suicide is more than a single, isolated behavior. Rather, self-destructive behaviors must fit into an overall pattern if we are truly to diagnose subtle suicide. This example helps drive home the point that things are often not what they appear. Applying the label "subtle suicide" to someone's behavior must be done cautiously.

The casual observer is likely to interpret self-defeating individuals as being lazy, self-destructive, depressed, lacking willpower, or having some type of abnormal personality. There is a natural tendency to make assumptions about the personality traits underlying others' behavior. Social psychologists call such explanations based on assumed personality traits the *fundamental attribution error*. This fancy term simply means that we are often wrong when we interpret someone else's behavior. After all, we rarely know others' backgrounds, the pressures they may be under, and the unique way they look at the world. Lacking information about a person that would help us understand the reasons for their behavior, we are likely to be wrong when we decide why someone is doing something—much more so when we don't know them well or when they don't talk to us about their feelings and circumstances.

This point is illustrated in the case of our overweight student Tom. We knew his circumstances and thus realized his overeating was not really indicative of subtle suicide tendencies. A stranger passing him on the street, however, might make quite a different and incorrect interpretation about why he had let himself get to such an obese state, thinking something like: "Look at that guy. He obviously doesn't care about himself or anyone else. He sure has low self-esteem and probably other psychological disorders and is trying to kill himself!"

Another biasing factor psychologists talk about is called the *just world explanation*. According to this notion, we often don't feel sorry for others' problems because we believe they are getting what they deserve. A common example is someone who says a rape victim who dressed seductively actually deserved to get raped—that it is clear she led her attacker on and is responsible for what happened. This type of blame-the-victim thinking also occurs when we see people engaging in self-destructive behavior. We assume they have some basic character flaws and decide they deserve whatever problems await them.

When you reach chapter 5, it will help if you remember these tendencies we all have when we judge others. The subtle suicide victim is especially difficult to deal with, and it is easy to let our frustrations and impatience lead us into faulty interpretations. Because it is easy to reach incorrect conclusions when we observe the behavior of others, it is important to obtain as much information as possible when we think we may be dealing with someone who is subtly suicidal. Self-destructive behavior patterns typical of subtle suicide can have varied causes, some of which we might not even imagine. Becoming aware of the causes of these patterns is a first step in understanding them. Furthermore, such understanding is crucial to finding effective ways of treating potentially life-threatening patterns of self-destruction.

CLASSIC EXAMPLES OF SUBTLE SUICIDE

In our opinion, the case involving our student did not meet the criteria for subtle suicide. Let's turn our attention now to a few others that we believe do meet the criteria. Using biographical data, let's explore some of what might be referred to as classic, and famous, examples of subtle suicide. Our analyses are much more condensed than available biographies because our interest is essentially confined to the subtle suicide process. We believe that this type of investigation will help readers relate more quickly and easily to our concept of subtle suicide. Later, we include many more examples of subtle suicide victims with whom we have been in direct contact, allowing us to feel even more confident that they fit our subtle suicide criteria.

Anna Nicole Smith

Anna Nicole Smith was born Vicky Lynn Hogan on November 28, 1967, in Houston, Texas. Her father was Donald Hogan, but Anna Nicole occasionally said that her purported mother, Virgie Hart, was not her real mom. She claimed that Virgie's younger sister, Kay Beall, was her real mother, not her aunt. Kay alleged that when she was ten years old and living with her sister, Donald Hogan raped her.

Virgie and Anna Nicole never got along well. According to Anna Nicole, Virgie was abusive and sometimes handcuffed her to a bed to keep her from moving about the house as children inevitably do. Anna Nicole's father, Donald, was not an integral part of her life, so she bounced between Virgie's and Kay's care throughout childhood.

Anna Nicole was a student at Durkee Elementary School and Aldine Intermediate School in Houston, before moving to Mexia, Texas, to attend high school. While in high school, she lived with her aunt, Kay. Unfortunately, living with her aunt did not afford conditions much better than those she experienced with her mom. Kay seemed dysfunctional as well. For example, she would have Anna Nicole steal toilet paper from a local restaurant because she said she could not afford to buy any of her own.

Melinda Hudson, Anna Nicole's cousin, described her as a "nerd" in high school. Anna Nicole admitted in a *Playboy* interview that she wasn't very popular in high school. Eventually she got into a fistfight with another student and was expelled. Subsequently, Anna Nicole worked at Jim's Crispy Fried Chicken. There, she had her eye on a sixteen-year-old cook, Billy Smith, who at first didn't show an interest in her. Eventually, she established a relationship with him and they had a son, Daniel. Anna Nicole claimed that Billy was a very jealous and abusive man, however, so she left him and moved back in with her mother, Virgie. Predictably, this living arrangement didn't last. Anna Nicole packed up her things, leaving baby Daniel with Virgie, and moved into a trailer park with a hairdresser she knew.

Anna Nicole needed money and serving at local restaurants was insufficient for her wants and needs. Thus, she started stripping at several exotic dancing bars. She had one of her managers hold some of the money she earned in order to save for breast implants. She frequently asked for withdrawals from her fund, most likely to feed her drug and alcohol habits. A coworker said that while she would go to her dances and talk to customers, he would have to hold her drugs for her so she would not lose them. Anna Nicole's drug of choice at the time was Xanax. It was common knowledge that she was embarrassed by the size of her feet and danced in shoes that were too small. A coworker who would rub her feet for her said that she ingested so much alcohol and Xanax that she would often just pass out during these massages. Not surprisingly, she was picked up for driving under the influence in Houston in 1989.

Her wild, risky behaviors didn't stop with drugs and alcohol. Anna Nicole's sexual behavior could be characterized as uninhibited, unrestrained, and out of control. She performed oral sex on numerous people in the strip clubs she worked, especially when money was thrown her way. She didn't care if others saw her engage in these acts or not. She also had an appetite for couple's sex, although she seemed to prefer women and dated many "dancers." Soon, she came up with money for her breast implants. According to one of her friends, a guy she was dating paid $8,000 for breast implants instead of buying her a car. Apparently, she could be quite persuasive when it came to getting what she desired. Eventually, at one of the clubs, she met J. Howard Marshall II, eighty-six years old and worth several hundred million dollars. They quickly became an "item," albeit an odd one.

Anna Nicole's main ambition was to become a high-fashion model. A response to an ad in Houston's edition of *Health and Fitness* magazine became her big break. She contacted Eric Reading to take Polaroid test shots for *Playboy*. Eventually, she became a *Playboy* centerfold in 1993 and was chosen as "Playmate of the Year." Around the same time, she was seeing both Howard Marshall and another man. It didn't take long for the other man to realize that Marshall was paying Anna for sexual favors. She didn't have a job, and the centerfold money was not enough to pay for her lifestyle. Allegedly, she aborted her boyfriend's baby because she didn't want Marshall to find out she was cheating on him.

Anna Nicole craved attention from both men and women. She flashed truckers on the highway just for a honk and a yell. Where was Daniel, her little boy, during these escapades? He was right beside her. Anna once said, "Daniel was used to hanging out with his mom." He was always included in the party. One day, while partying, she whipped off her blouse and allowed both men and women strangers to fondle her in front of her son and colleagues. She justified this type of behavior by saying that if she treated Daniel like an adult and kept him around adult situations, he would grow up faster. An example of how aggressive she could be in pursuing women was represented in a judgment of several hundred thousand dollars that she was required to pay to a former maid because of assault and sexual harassment.

According to reports, she was capable of drinking an entire bottle of tequila on her own. She sometimes ingested Vicodin and Xanax like they were candy. She drank almost daily, liked painkillers, and sometimes added Ecstasy. Food was another pleasure she could not moderate well. As a result, she had two liposuction procedures. It was not uncommon for her to binge, purge, and take great quantities of laxatives. Anna Nicole also used cocaine to help diminish her appetite. She admitted that her body size made her feel depressed. Obviously, becoming obese did not help her feel better about living.

Ultimately, Anna Nicole married Howard Marshall in 1994. After a small reception, she patted him on the head and waved good-bye while taking the arm of her former boyfriend, Pierre Dejean. On August 4, 1995, Marshall died at the age of ninety.

A few months later, Anna overdosed once again by mixing alcohol, painkillers, and tranquilizers. She checked into the Betty Ford Clinic. There was some talk of permanent brain damage after this overdose, but no public statement of this type was put forth. However, those who saw her subsequently on television and in person were often struck by how her personality seemed to have changed. On September 7, 2006, she had a daughter named Danny Lynn Hope. Just three days after the birth of her daughter, her son Daniel died suddenly. Lab tests found Lexapro, Zoloft, and Methadone in his system. Anna Nicole herself died of an overdose on February 8, 2007.

Retrospective analysis of Anna Nicole's life evokes a wide variety of images and emotions, mostly negative. Her death and her son's, together with Danny Lynn now being motherless, leads us to envision a wasteland of human potential. What could have been a bountiful harvest of love and achievement is now dead.

As a child, Anna Nicole seemed to have no real connection with others, and this pattern continued into adulthood. As an adult, she moved from one superficial relationship to another while both blatantly using others and being used. She constantly numbed herself with alcohol and numerous drugs and medications so she didn't have to feel painful emotions and realities, including rejection, abuse, and low self-esteem.

Ultimately, like many before her, her death was ruled "accidental." We will never really know for sure whether she wanted to die or simply didn't care whether she lived or died. Nevertheless, it doesn't appear to be a stretch to conclude that Anna Nicole Smith passed into the subtle suicide zone at some point and never exited it for long thereafter. Her extensive history of self-destructive behaviors in many forms buttresses this notion. She provided clear examples of continuous reckless and dangerous behavior patterns, despite the fact that she had the resources and opportunities to exit this pathway and enter a more constructive lifestyle. Although many adored and even envied her, it was not enough to fill her emptiness. Perhaps the death of her son was the final straw. Even the birth of her daughter was not enough motivation to change her self-defeating/destructive acts. When her son died, it appears Anna Nicole lost the only person she ever loved, even if not in a mature fashion.

Marilyn Monroe

Marilyn Monroe was born Norma Jean Mortenson on June 1, 1926. Just two weeks after her birth, her mother gave her to a foster family because she believed she was unsuitable to be a parent. Norma Jean told a friend years later that her mother didn't want her. She felt she got in her mother's way and was a disgrace to her. Her mother visited every now and then, but less so as time passed.

Marilyn recalled that in her foster home, no one ever called her pretty. She was raised in a very religious and strict home where she didn't feel good enough and was continually told that she could do better. She was taught that dancing, smoking, and acting in movies were the devil's doings.

When Marilyn was seven, her mother took her out of the foster home and decided to raise her on her own. Her mother spent most nights doing the things Marilyn had been taught were works of the devil. Her mother was treated for depression about a year later. Clearly, there was a lack of stability and consistency in her early upbringing.

When she was nine, Marilyn was sent to an orphanage and stayed there until she was eleven. Around this time, her moods seemed to darken. She recalled that she was never happy during these years. She was sent to another home but wasn't there long because of being sexually abused by the male of the house.

Marilyn had a very unstable childhood that she recalled as very confusing. The next home she lived in was with a great aunt and three cousins. Norma Jean was once again sexually assaulted by one of her cousins. This incident reinforced her sense that she was desired primarily as a sexual object. She was taken out of this home and sent to her mother's best friend's aunt.

Marilyn was shy and withdrawn during this phase and had very few friends at school. At thirteen, she grew to her full height of five-foot-five-and-a-half.

She developed earlier than most girls. In high school, Marilyn found it hard to apply herself because she was distracted by the presence of a twenty-year-old man who lived across the street. They began dating, and understandably she became very emotionally dependent on him. At sixteen, she dropped out of school and married him. She called him "Daddy" and considered him more of a father and protector than a husband. He joined the Merchant Marine, where his job was to train recruits.

Later, an Army photographer taking pictures for the Army newspapers and magazines met Marilyn, and she quickly became known as a photographer's dream. The pictures he took of her were the first of her to appear in publication. Her husband did not approve of her modeling, however, and told her that she could only have one career and that a woman cannot be two places at once. At nineteen, after three years of marriage and two affairs with photographers, she filed for divorce.

Marilyn believed she didn't have any friends. She had teachers and people she could look up to, but she always felt that she was a nobody. The only way she thought she could be *somebody* was to be somebody *else,* which is probably why she wanted to act. At the age of twenty, Marilyn signed with one of the largest motion picture studios, Twentieth Century-Fox, as Norma Jean Dougherty. However, her name had to be changed because no one was sure how her last name should be pronounced.

Initially, things did not go well, and money was in short supply. Often, Marilyn would go without eating just to pay for acting lessons. She believed that doing so was good for her figure. She put all her money into classes, rent, and auto maintenance. She got food by offering herself for quick sex with men in cars on side streets near Hollywood or Santa Monica Boulevard. In 1949, Marilyn posed for what became a world-famous nude calendar picture. It was this photo that Hugh Hefner bought and used to launch his first issue of *Playboy.*

While experiencing two more failing marriages, one to New York Yankees legend Joe DiMaggio and the other to a famous playwright, Arthur Miller, Marilyn's life continued to spiral downward. She developed a serious habit of taking sleeping pills that began in early 1954. Use of hypnotics and barbiturates led to her occasional dangerous combinations of these pills and wine that disturbed what little routine she had and made her moody and lethargic the next day. These drugs caused depression, confusion, and incoherent speech. She also suffered from horrible nightmares, unpredictable mood changes, and rashes.

For much of the winter of 1961, Marilyn stayed at home in her darkened bedroom, played sentimental records, sedated herself with pills, and rapidly lost weight. A friend suggested that she check into a private ward of New York Hospital for a physical workup and rest. Purportedly, she was placed in a locked and padded room, one of the cells for the most disturbed patients. Marilyn was later taken out of the hospital and agreed to enter a far more comfortable and less threatening environment at Columbia University, Presbyterian Hospital Medical Center. She remained there for several weeks and regained her strength.

Allegedly, she became sexually involved with President John F. Kennedy in 1962. Involvements with many other notable figures have been reported elsewhere. With Marilyn's risky and careless behavior patterns, it was only a matter of time before something tragic would happen. On August 4, 1962, she was found lying motionless in her bed. The preliminary report from the Office of the County Coroner on August 10 stated that her death occurred because of a possible overdose of barbiturates. On August 17, this was changed to a probable suicide. On August 27, the final statement reported that her death resulted from barbiturate overdose. There were no external signs of violence.

We will never know whether Marilyn Monroe intentionally killed herself or "accidentally" overdosed during a drug-induced stupor. What we do know is that she lived a life full of acclaim and adoration by millions of fans and admirers. Yet, she was never capable of accepting the attention and praise of those who looked up to her in so many ways. Even with all of the successes that are associated with being a movie star, she displayed evidence of low self-esteem, emotional instability, marked insecurities, and self-destructive behavior patterns. Whether she committed overt suicide or not, those close to her were not surprised by her demise. They could see a tragedy coming from miles away.

Marilyn showed numerous signs of lack of respect for her body and well-being. She also showed clear evidence of a strong need to numb herself to psychological realities with powerful medications. She gave indications of not being comfortable with herself or enjoying life on a routine basis. Considering these observations and impressions, it is not surprising that Marilyn died at such a young age and in such an avoidable fashion. It is difficult to escape the conclusion that her life as a child and adolescent set her on the road to subtle suicide.

There are interesting similarities between Marilyn Monroe's life and Anna Nicole Smith's, although some of the similarities appear to be more by design than coincidence, because Anna Nicole obviously tried to emulate Marilyn in many ways. Nevertheless, Marilyn's life did parallel Anna Nicole's to some degree. History suggests both grew up with a lack of unconditional love in their primary environment. Both had difficulty maintaining intimate relationships during adulthood. Despite having many adoring fans, neither appeared to develop emotional stability or a positive sense of self. Both gave the impression that their self-worth was essentially associated with their youth and physical appearance. Both seemed driven to engage in risky behaviors and the self-numbing use of psychiatric medications to avoid feeling guilt, shame, anxiety, depression, and other negative emotions that were natural responses to their environmental histories. Finally, both suffered a similar fate: death at their own hands, accidental or otherwise.

Although their similarities are blatant, we see major differences as well. We might describe Anna Nicole as a "poor man's" Marilyn. Although not the best at her craft, Marilyn could sing, act, and dance. She didn't marry someone more than fifty years older. Furthermore, we have no evidence she used plastic surgery to alter her body. Most importantly, perhaps, she did not abandon an infant child with her self-destructive behaviors. She wasn't as childlike with her behaviors and was intimate with and married to persons of much higher acclaim. Marilyn was an international movie star who indirectly carried the banner of the United States. The same could not be said for Anna Nicole.

We make these points because we want to emphasize that people of very different personalities and maturity levels can be subtly suicidal. Yet, in the final analysis it didn't matter. Both Anna Nicole Smith and Marilyn Monroe succumbed to the demons of their youth after passing through the subtle suicide zone.

Evel Knievel

Robert Craig Knievel, better known as Evel Knievel, was born on October 17, 1938, in Butte, Montana. Butte was a rugged frontier mining boomtown that was home to the Anaconda Copper Mining Company, where many of the city's residents were employed. Given the nature of the time and the fact that the community was employed in such dangerous work, people tended to engage in many risk-taking behaviors such as drinking, gambling, and prostitution.

When Evel was eighteen months old, his parents divorced. His father moved to California and his mother to Nevada. As a result, Evel and his siblings were raised by their grandparents. When he was eight, Evel set the stage for his daredevil future. After seeing an inspiring performance by Joey Chitwood, who was a talented auto daredevil of the time, Evel and his brother Nic decided to remove their grandfather's garage doors to use them as bicycle ramps. Both boys rounded up the neighborhood children and put on a show for those willing to pay two cents each. When jumping his bicycle wasn't enough, Evel's brother gathered weeds and lit them on fire between the garage doors so Evel could jump through the flames. This was the first of several unsuccessful jumps in his career, and the crash ended in both doors burning.

When Evel was ten, he heard a train coming and climbed up on a trestle. After seeing a man in a white suit and top hat, he waited for the last car to pass and jumped on the caboose to shake his hand. The man turned out to be President Harry Truman.

In addition to jumping his bicycle, Evel raced soapbox cars and built small roller coasters. For fun, he and his friends threw rocks at prostitutes until they were chased away by pimps. In high school, he ran track and played ice hockey, but he excelled at the more extreme sport of ski jumping and won the Northern Rocky Mountain Ski Association Class A men's ski jumping championship in 1957. At age fifteen, he visited his father, who had a new wife and three daughters in California. (His mother had also remarried and had two new daughters.) During Evel's visit, his father bought him his first motorcycle. A year later, he dropped out of high school and started getting into trouble committing various crimes such as reckless motorcycling, vandalism, fighting, and stealing purses and hubcaps. He apparently was given his nickname when stealing hubcaps from a family friend who called him an "evil Knievel."

In 1956, Evel's father moved back to Butte with his wife and kids. Instead of working at his father's Volkswagen dealership, Evel chose to work in the mines as a diamond drill operator and skip tender. In addition, he drove his coworkers around in a company bus, but later stopped due to complaints about his wild driving. He was eventually fired after hitting power lines that caused a blackout in the town. As a result, Evel enlisted in the Army in the late 1950s, where among other things, he was involved in pole-vaulting.

Around this time, Evel met his future wife, Linda, who was seventeen. Her parents disapproved of their relationship, which led him to feel he had to "kidnap" Linda so they could elope. His plan to whisk Linda away and marry her was foiled, however, when they were stopped by the highway patrol. He eventually got his way in 1959 when he and Linda were officially married.

With three children and a wife to support, Evel moved from one job to the next, including rodeo riding and motorcycle racing. He even thought he could play professional hockey, but his semipro career was short-lived. Evel had trouble keeping respectable jobs. He had some success as an insurance agent and asked to be promoted to vice president where he worked. When he wasn't afforded such a position, he quit.

Evel tended to become enthralled with get-rich-quick schemes and self-help books. When his schemes inevitably fell through, he reportedly robbed banks, grocery stores, and pharmacies. He even bragged that he could crack a safe in two minutes with one hand behind his back. He supposedly claimed that the cops knew what he was doing but couldn't prove it. Evel is said to have compared the feeling he received when stealing from a bank with the one he had when about to perform a motorcycle jump.

He began to see that there were some disadvantages to his antisocial behavior patterns. Working with several mobsters, Evel witnessed one get killed by the police. At this point, he realized he could end up in prison, addicted to drugs, or dead. He claimed that criminal behaviors made him feel suicidal and led to a "nervous breakdown" at twenty-five.

Evel returned to motorcycle racing after becoming a partner in a Honda motorcycle dealership. When money was short, he decided to jump a pen of venomous rattlesnakes. He was just short on his forty-foot attempt, causing the pen to break open and the snakes to slither out into the crowd. Evel laughed and said he knew he could draw a big crowd by jumping over weird stuff.

Some of Evel's career highlights include successfully jumping over fifty stacked cars, up to thirteen Mack trucks, and as many as fourteen Greyhound buses. However, some of his most famous jumps were unsuccessful, such as the one over the fountains at Caesars Palace in Las Vegas that left him with many serious injuries and put him in a coma for twenty-nine days. Prior to this jump, he engaged in some self-promotion by calling the executive director of Caesars Palace on several occasions, each time pretending to represent a large corporation or media organization and asking the director if he knew anything about Evel Knievel in order to make his name familiar and spark some interest in this supposedly fascinating character.

When Evel couldn't get permission to jump across the Grand Canyon, he decided to jump the Snake River Canyon instead. Due to strong winds, his parachute carried him back into the canyon, and he crashed several feet from the raging river. Spectators thought for sure he was going to die, but he survived and cheated death once again. He seemed to believe his competitive spirit and killer instinct could always beat his toughest competitor, Death—either that or he didn't give a damn if he died!

The jump that ended Evel's career and caused him to retire took place in Chicago in 1980. In an attempt to jump over a tank full of sharks, he crashed and his motorcycle hit a cameraman, causing the man to lose an eye. Evel was rushed to the hospital with a concussion and broken forearm.

Evel always scoffed at his injuries. He said in various interviews that except for his neck, he had broken every bone in his body at least once. He had about thirty-five or forty screws in him to hold bones together, and all of his hospital time just blurred together. Although Evel had trouble recalling his hospital stays, staff remembered him well. He was a very demanding patient, often complaining of such things as the food being bad and the nurses being ugly.

Coming from a humble upbringing in Montana, Evel welcomed attention and fame with open arms and lived a lavish lifestyle. He attended celebrity gatherings and dropped names of famous individuals, often commenting that they were dear friends even if they were only acquaintances. He spent most of the money earned throughout his career on himself through excessive gambling and indulging in nothing but the best, from expensive cars to clothing and jewelry. He wore large diamond rings on both of his hands. In addition, he wore gold watches, chains, and bracelets. His attire made him look like a pimp, which he had aspired to be as a child.

One of Evel's favorite activities was golf, and he often bet thousands of dollars while playing a single round. He even went as far as betting the tip of his finger on a single putt. He lost this bet and chopped off the tip of his finger with a shovel, later having it sewn back on. Reportedly, he also once bet thirty thousand dollars on a game of blackjack.

In addition to his gambling habit, Evel consumed a fifth of Wild Turkey bourbon daily for years. Those closest to him were deeply affected by his mood swings. His drinking was a factor in his womanizing, excessive wild partying, and weight gain. In an interview, his wife Linda said that times with Evel at the height of his fame were the unhappiest years of her life because he was mean when he was drinking. She claimed she tried doing what she could to make him happy, but eventually she realized she could not please him, so she just quit trying.

Throughout these years, Evel was convicted of several felonies and faced arrests and misdemeanors. He assaulted a cameraman and had a warrant out for his arrest in Fort Lauderdale, Florida, for "battery and criminal mischief." In 1964, there were arrests for disorderly conduct, along with others involving bad checks. Then, in 1977, Evel assaulted and beat author Sheldon Saltman with a baseball bat, accusing Saltman of writing lies about him; Saltman suffered a compound fracture of his left arm and a broken right wrist.

Evel was arrested on felony assault charges after the Saltman attack. He drank half a bottle of Wild Turkey before each of his court appearances and made no attempt to dress conservatively to create a positive image. In court, he admitted to his premeditated attack and pleaded guilty while showing no remorse. He was sentenced to six months in a Los Angeles County jail and three years' probation and was fined more than a million dollars in damages. Nevertheless, he reported up to his death that he never paid the fine, and on several occasions, he said that he was not sorry for his actions.

In 1995, Evel was diagnosed with hepatitis C that was thought to be the result of a tainted blood transfusion. The condition was undoubtedly complicated by his toxic levels of alcohol consumption. He was given less than five years to live. Fortunately, four years and some months later, in January 1999, Evel received a new liver from an organ donor. Only weeks later, however, doctors discovered that the hepatitis had taken over his body once again.

In the last years of his life, Evel Knievel, once able to jump thirteen Mack trucks with his motorcycle, had trouble doing simple tasks such as getting up to answer the phone. As a matter of fact, the last time he attempted to ride a motorcycle, he snapped his ankle. He lived in pain while hooked up to oxygen and a drug pump that was inserted to his abdomen to deliver morphine and synthetic heroin. In addition, he suffered from the effects of a stroke and was at high risk for pulmonary fibrosis. Although he could no longer perform motorcycle jumps, he continued to get some type of satisfaction from gambling. He bet on most NFL games during the season and admitted that he didn't plan to give that up anytime soon. He died on November 30, 2007.

Evel Knievel grew up without the nurturance, acceptance, and support most children get. He learned to put little stock in people and relationships. Rather, he developed strong motivations to confront challenges and achieve material successes, as well as a lot of approval and attention from the larger community. At the same time, he displayed an unusually powerful desire to challenge death. It was as though he was compelled to risk his life and lifestyle with daredevil acts, alcohol consumption, womanizing, criminal activities, gambling, and other self-destructive behavior patterns. All of this demonstrates the deep ambivalence he felt about living, consciously or otherwise.

Amazingly, for years he survived to live another day, although he became a shell of the man he once was. Just about every bone in his body had been broken at least once. Although the length of his life may not have been altered much by his self-destructive tendencies, his later years were anything but "golden." Thus, the quality of his life was permanently damaged. This fact shows a significant aspect of our definition of subtle suicide. People do not always die prematurely from subtle suicide. Sometimes it is the quality of life that is significantly damaged, even if they die of causes unrelated to the subtle suicide process.

Jim Morrison

Jim Morrison was an American singer, songwriter, and poet, front man of the Doors, and one of the most charismatic figures in the history of rock music. He broke ground with complex songs about sex, drugs, mysticism, murder, madness, and self-destruction. He is known for his provocative behavior and excesses of alcohol and drugs. Unfortunately, Jim's rockstar lifestyle led to his death at the age of twenty-seven. His premature death has been the subject of much speculation. At the center of this controversy is the question of whether it was accidental or intentional. Nevertheless, we feel a subtle suicide analysis of his life will help teach us some important lessons. With that in mind, we will investigate some relevant aspects of his brief but infamous life.

Jim Morrison was born in Florida in 1943. His father was in the military and was away in World War II during his early life. His family, which consisted of his parents and younger brother and sister, led a nomadic lifestyle. Jim's parents did not believe in corporal punishment of their children. Instead, they administered punishment via "dressing down," a military tradition of verbal abuse. They would yell and berate the children until they were reduced to tears. According to his younger brother, Jim never shed a tear.

One of the most profound moments in Jim Morrison's life, the subject of many songs and poems, occurred during a road trip with his family when he was five years of age. They had come across an accident in New Mexico with Indians bleeding to death on the road. Frightened, Jim claimed he saw the ghost of the Indians running frantically around the scene, and one of them entered his body. His parents tried to calm him down and told him it was only a bad dream. Real or imagined, it had a major impact on his life and writings.

In the Doors' first album, released in 1967, Jim falsely declared that his parents and siblings were dead. He had been out of communication with them after having an argument with his dad over his musical talent. Before his rise to stardom, he had begun experimenting with drugs, taking copious amounts of LSD and alcohol. He reportedly began showing up late and inebriated for recording sessions and live performances. By 1969, he had gained more than twenty pounds because of his alcohol use. That same year, he was convicted of indecent exposure and public profanity after inciting a riot among a crowd at a concert. Jim's apathy and indulgence came out in his relationships, too. Before becoming successful, he met his long-term companion, Pam Courson. They had an "open relationship," with many loud arguments and periods of separation. At the time of his death, it was determined that they qualified as a common-law marriage.

In 1970, Jim took part in a pagan "handfasting" ceremony with another woman during which they declared themselves married. However, none of the necessary paperwork was filed for the union to be considered legal. Also, he had sexual interactions with fans and a number of short flings with celebrities, most of which were one-night stands. At the time of his death, there were allegedly twenty paternity actions pending against him.

Jim Morrison's death on July 3, 1971, was somewhat of a shock, considering he was so young and successful. He had moved to Paris that year to take a break from performing and concentrate on his writing. While there, he shed a great deal of excess weight, shaved his beard, and made an attempt to clean up his life. It has been said that he intended to patch things up with his father, as well. However, it appeared that he became depressed while there and began showing symptoms of congestive heart failure, most likely the result of excessive drug use. The morning after he died, he was found in a bathtub with dried blood around his nose and mouth and a huge bruise on his chest. Although many rumors circulated that he had overdosed on heroin and some said he died from a massive hemorrhage caused by tuberculosis, the official report listed cause of death as heart failure. Because no autopsy was done, his death is still somewhat of a mystery.

Whether Jim Morrison used hallucinogenic substances as an escape from reality or as a portal to deeper thoughts, the origins of such use seemed rooted in his childhood experiences. In order to deal with the pressure and inconsistency of constantly changing homes, as well as coping with verbal abuse, he had to find a way to disappear inside of himself and find some kind of comfort from within. It is tempting to simply dismiss him as just another drug user who died from an addiction. However, this explanation ignores his successes, talent, and creativity. There are unique aspects to his life that we believe illuminate relevant aspects of our subtle suicide concept.

Jim Morrison acted with disdain for both social convention and his own health and well-being. Such unconventional and rebellious actions suggest a great deal of unresolved anger. For whatever reasons, he did not act like he cared about living a long or healthy life. Rather, he chose to live fast and furious while courting death, despite becoming an American icon in the music industry. As we saw in the classic examples earlier, we can't fill up a psychological tank that doesn't accept recognition, approval, love, and acceptance as fuel. Unfortunately, it seems obvious that Jim was a lost soul. He simply could not feel secure in love, no matter how others responded to him. Like our other classic cases, we see evidence that self-destructive individuals typically reject and repudiate those who love and accept them. As a result, no one wins.

Where does this pattern originate? Once again, there is information available that childhood and adolescence are vulnerable periods for development of subtle suicide patterns. Interestingly, this pattern can become so powerful that it overrides our built-in desire to survive. The effects of childhood damage may take many years if not decades to come to fruition. As a result, we may not see the linkage between things that happened in the earlier years and their tragic results until it is too late.

We can certainly argue that the self-destructive person's desire to live is simply reduced by temporary drug-induced states that lower inhibitions and judgment. This type of argument ignores the fact that such individuals usually have been in these states many times. A person who truly wants to live and carry on a life of purpose and meaning will be frightened enough to avoid these types of experiences. In other words, self-destructive people make choices that lead to repeating exposure to states of altered consciousness that are actually near-death experiences. The reality is that this does not sufficiently frighten a person in the subtle suicide zone. Why? Because they simply do not care enough about living. Simply put, they don't have both feet in life. At best, they have one foot in. Life is hard enough even when we're totally committed to it. When we're only partially committed, however, it is easier to be buried in an avalanche of stressors and responsibilities.

LIFE IS HELL, BUT ...

If I genuinely want to kill myself, is it really that difficult to complete this act? Probably not. However, according to estimates, for every individual who "successfully" completes the act, there are eight to ten others who make an unsuccessful attempt. What are we to make of this information? Actually, we find the discrepancy quite consistent with experiences in treating both psychiatric inpatient and outpatient clients, and with the concept of subtle suicide. The fact is that most suicidal people are not sold on the idea of killing themselves. They are, in fact, quite ambivalent about the act and may suffer from subtle suicide. They hope someone or something will help turn their life around in a positive way, thus allowing them to be more certain about their purpose and roles in life.

Based on conversations with sufferers, we believe there are several reasons why subtly suicidal people tend to stay in a "dead zone" between living and dying and avoid serious efforts to kill themselves:

- *Death anxiety.* They voice anxiety due to the uncertainty of what happens after death. Although they are not satisfied with life, their fear of death overpowers the desire to commit overt suicide.
- *Concept of hell.* Many of the people we have interviewed speak of their religiously driven belief that suicide would condemn them to hell forever. Once again, this fear dominates their wish to commit overt suicide.
- *Effects on others.* Many subtle suicide victims say they cannot commit suicide because the act would devastate their loved ones. We don't find this motivation in every subtly suicidal victim, though; some, in fact, seem almost oblivious to the damage they inflict on those around them.
- *Fear of an unsuccessful attempt.* A small number of clients, a distinct minority, describe anxiety over being disabled or in a vegetative state if their preferred method of suicide does not work. The thought of this outcome horrifies them enough to keep them from trying to commit overt suicide.

Note that these four factors are not mutually exclusive. Therefore, the subtly suicidal may be affected by any number of these factors at various points in time.

We believe that many people who are preoccupied with overt suicide are really victims of subtle suicide. They want to stay alive, but also want to die. In order to be treated successfully, these victims need to be confronted about their deep ambivalence toward living. The conflicts within this type of individual, however, run deep and require special attention and effort. Therapy will be difficult because people who don't consistently care about living are not likely to agree to psychotherapy or medication. We cannot simply assume that these individuals will be committed to interventions and treatment goals.

For clients who are ambivalent about whether they want to be alive or not, it is also difficult to sustain motivation to improve their thoughts and actions. Some clients, particularly hospitalized ones, routinely question whether they want to be alive, and fail to improve. As a result, therapists and caretakers become frustrated with lack of continued progress and may even blame clients for treatment failures. Such clients are often considered resistant, and family, friends, and professionals give up on them because they make little progress and do not seem to be consistently motivated to improve their lives. A better understanding of the underlying psychological states allows us to see that ambivalence about living undermines clients' motivation to get better and can lead to a vicious cycle of self-defeating and self-destructive actions and thoughts.

THE SUBTLE SUICIDE ZONE

Most people do not experience long-term ambivalence about being alive. However, many individuals have been self-destructive, experienced significant depression, and even entertained occasional suicidal thoughts at some point. A number of these people move on to experience the process of subtle suicide, a very destructive and potentially lethal process. Once the process takes hold, it is difficult to escape. Lack of awareness and sustained motivation to change self-destructive behavior patterns will usually lead to devastating effects for the affected individual and others around him or her. The person enters what we call a "subtle suicide zone," and once trapped there, it is difficult to exit. A pattern of self-destructive and self-defeating behavioral patterns inevitably follows, creating a type of psychological prison. Once in this zone, individuals may take years to spiral downward or could do so in a relatively brief period of time. Victims vary in their degree of awareness of the process. Similar to overtly suicidal individuals, a kind of tunnel vision occurs. That is, subtle suicidal victims usually have difficulty seeing the "big picture." They typically lack clarity and insight into how self-defeating and self-destructive they are and where their patterns of behavior are taking them. They truly become the living dead.

The subtle suicide client presents considerable challenges to health-care workers. We find that the attitudes of human service providers involved in treating this kind of client often deteriorate quickly from empathy to insensitivity and blaming. Consistent with the just world explanation mentioned at the beginning of this chapter, these attitudes underscore a tendency to believe that people get what they deserve. Therefore, subtle suicide clients are likely to be seen as deserving their lot in life. This belief makes it hard for health-care practitioners to feel much sympathy for the client, and the client is blamed for frustrations felt by the health-care workers themselves. The providers feel helpless because of their inability to help alleviate their client's suffering. It is understandable that many health-care professionals give in to the tendency to blame the client and provide less effort to help them; after all, the providers begin to feel they are wasting efforts on those who don't care enough to help themselves.

The problem here is that the health-care worker is not versed in the dynamics of the subtle suicide client. The worker, in fact, is operating under a model that says clients need to be motivated to help make their therapy work; clients must be willing to take on personal responsibility and work diligently to change their lives for the better. The subtle suicide client, however, does not show these characteristics to a sufficient degree, so they are blamed for not caring and being unwilling to change; clients are simply seen as lazy, irresponsible, resistant, or immature. We might point out that these reactions are typical not only of mental health providers; they also occur in friends and family members of the subtle suicide victim, who constantly struggle to help someone who really doesn't seem to care very much about life.

Although it is certainly understandable, we think much of this blame and criticism of the sufferer is inappropriate, because the subtle suicide client has issues that go much deeper than the typical client who is suffering from anxiety, depression, and other psychological disorders. If we stop and think about it, who really wants to suffer from a deep ambivalence about living? Who wants to continue engaging in self-defeating and self-destructive acts? We certainly don't hear young people discuss such tendencies as goals in their lives.

We think many of the individuals who are ultimately blamed by family, friends, and practitioners for their problems in adjustment are actually displaying strong symptoms of subtle suicide. Furthermore, in the case of subtle suicide, we believe we are most likely dealing with individuals who don't deserve to be blamed for their psychological problems. Both overtly suicidal and subtly suicidal individuals possess genetic and environmental factors that have interacted to produce their maladaptive functioning. Whether overtly or subtly suicidal, anyone who makes suicidal gestures and ends up locked in a psychiatric ward has some serious psychological issues!

We humans are acutely aware of life and death. We know we will die. However, we also know we can influence the timing and cause of our death if we so choose. Thus, we need to want to live more than to die or else we will likely become self-neglecting, self-defeating, and maybe even self-destructive. Life is stressful enough when we want to live. Imagine how difficult it is when we are ambivalent about living. Thus, a sustained state of ambivalence about living, just like a sincere desire to die, will make us defenseless against ourselves. We can become our own worst enemy, lose the will to survive, and ultimately spiral down a continuous path of self-defeating and self-destructive actions.

OVERT VERSUS SUBTLE SUICIDE

The act of suicide is one of the most profound and puzzling events of human experience. It is difficult to get accurate statistics of actual suicides because there may be sketchy evidence of what actually happened, or the person committing the act may have masked the real intent by simulating an accident or a naturally occurring experience. In fact, it has been estimated that suicides may really be two to four times higher than the number officially reported.

Although many contemplate suicide, only a small number seriously make the attempt. For those who have witnessed suicide or known someone intimately who has committed such an act, the experience is typically devastating and has long-term effects. Understandably, seeing someone jump off a bridge or building, hang from a rope, or with a gunshot to the head leaves vivid and disturbing mental pictures.

Overt suicide has long been a main focus of psychological research and theory, for three reasons. First, the dramatic nature of suicide makes it indelibly imprinted in our minds. Second, we are able to generate statistics of how many suicides are committed each year and can break them down by age, ethnicity, gender, and other characteristics. Thus, it is relatively easy to associate overt suicide with such factors as socioeconomic and marital status, race, and ethnicity. Third, efforts to discover the relationship between suicide and other relevant variables can help with prevention and treatment of suicidal behavior and thus benefit countless individuals.

Compared to overt suicide, subtle suicide is grossly underestimated in frequency and impact. As a matter of fact, this pattern of behavior is not widely studied at all. The reasons are fairly obvious. Subtle suicide is more passive, more covert, and, well, more subtle than overt suicide. But whatever the reasons, we think the neglect of subtle suicide in psychological research and theory is unfortunate. We believe subtle suicide is more common than overt suicide and has extremely negative effects upon the self-perpetrators, their significant others, and society at large.

For comparison purposes, we can consider subtle suicide as analogous to psychological abuse and neglect, and overt suicide as analogous to physical or sexual abuse. Although psychological abuse is more complex and ambiguous, and more difficult to define and determine when it has occurred, do we want to say that psychological abuse is less important to one's health than physical or sexual abuse? Shouldn't we try to define, diagnose, prevent, and treat the effects of psychological abuse? Isn't it possible that psychological abuse is more prevalent and ultimately more harmful to individuals and society than physical or sexual abuse, particularly because it may go undetected and untreated for so long?

In fact, many clients and students have told us they preferred physical abuse to psychological abuse as children and adolescents. Compared to psychological abuse, they agree that physical and sexual abuse is less personally harmful. These latter forms of abuse are also usually easy to identify through medical examination and easy to get statistics on. Like overt suicide, there is more focus on physical or sexual abuse than psychological abuse in textbooks, children's and youth agencies, the legal system, and the media. But this preoccupation with the physical and sexual often pushes psychological abuse, not to mention a condition like subtle suicide, off the radar when we deal with troubled people.

Our society has become obsessed with overt suicide. The media splash front-page articles and television reports of murder-suicides, mass suicides, terrorist suicide attacks, copycat suicides, and doctor-assisted suicides. Most cities have suicide hotlines and help centers, and psychiatric hospitals are filled with clients who have attempted suicide, some of them many times.

A great deal of time, effort, and money is spent on keeping alive people who have expressed suicidal ideas or made actual attempts. These efforts are understandable. However, we believe this concentration on overt suicide prevention and treatment has masked the incidence of subtle suicide, a huge problem for society that brings untold psychological pain and death. Deterrence of overt suicide stresses quantity of life, but we also need to focus on quality of life.

Textbooks on abnormal psychology include extensive and detailed coverage of overt suicide, possibly even an entire chapter. The mention of passive tendencies along the lines of what we call subtle suicide, however, is likely to be found nowhere in these textbooks. Why? The simplest explanation would be that this is an entirely new concept. However, while we would like to say that our concept of subtle suicide is completely novel, that would be untrue. There are a number of theorists and researchers in this area of study who have set the stage for this work. Although subtle suicide does not have an overwhelming foundation of research and theory, there is a distinct body of knowledge that allows for advancement of a coherent set of hypotheses and theories related to this important concept. To the best of our knowledge, however, our definition and formal use of the term *subtle suicide* to describe a syndrome is new.

We also believe subtle suicide has been largely ignored because it is complicated and hard to identify. Unlike overt suicide, the subtle kind is much more difficult to observe, define, and study. We live in a society in love with statistics—teachers and employers use tests to evaluate performance, colleges and graduate schools use SATs, GREs, and LSATs as criteria for admission—so it is difficult to get people to pay attention to concepts or issues that are difficult to quantify. It is much easier to get the attention and support of government and private agencies for more quantifiable and recognizable problems like child abuse and alcoholism.

When was the last time you heard of someone getting a ticket for tailgating? This behavior is more difficult to identify and prosecute than is speeding, which police can easily measure using radar. Yet, is tailgating really so irrelevant? We think not. The distinction between overt speeding and subtle tailgating is similar to a basic idea of this book: although subtle suicide is a difficult process to define and investigate, we should not ignore or minimize it. The more vague nature of subtle suicide does not make it less important to study and treat.

Whether suicide is committed in a passive and gradual fashion or in an active and overt manner, it is not against the law in the United States. In fact, it may even be a rational choice made by the individual. Without getting into a long philosophical discussion here, there is obviously a major difference between *forcing* a person to do what we think is in their best interest and *helping to prevent* them from doing self-harm. Frankly, it isn't our life and we don't have to "live in the other's shoes." Moreover, if people are hell-bent on suicide, let's be honest: no one can stop them. However, we believe we all have the responsibility and ability to positively confront people who are in the subtle suicide zone, just as we do with those who are overtly suicidal.

_____ *Chapter 3* _____

Subtle Suicide Dynamics: Case Studies

Just as there are many causes of cancer, heart disease, and other ailments, we have seen many pathways to subtle suicide. Actually, each case involves unique combinations of genetic and environmental influences. When looking at individual cases, therefore, it is important to remember that even though we look for and prefer simple answers to complex issues, in truth there are none. Thus, we are left with the reality of trying to explain a very complex and baffling phenomenon.

The causes and effects of some cases are "relatively" simple. In other words, there are more or less clear precipitating factors (e.g., quick onset due to devastating and obvious losses) and consistent behavioral effects (e.g., social withdrawal, aggression). On the other hand, in most cases, we see gradual onset due to multiple causes (e.g., a lifetime of emotional deprivation), along with multiple effects (e.g., eating disorders, sexual dysfunction, depression, and medication abuse).

To help simplify this complex process, we have chosen to highlight in separate cases what we view as the predominant causes of the subtle suicide process. We realize there are typically many causative factors that interact in complex fashion to produce such a process. However, we feel that organizing our discussions in this manner helps clarify what we see as the most common psychological causes of subtle suicide.

In chapter 1, we noted that risks, vulnerabilities, potentiators, and protectors are all involved in the development of subtle suicide. In presenting case studies, we will emphasize the primary role of risk factors. However, vulnerabilities, potentiators, and protectors will also be noticeably present and included. We will note causative factors unique to adults, such as job-related stress and accidents, taking responsibility for elderly parents, spousal abuse, and raising or taking care of psychiatrically or physically disabled family members. Our cases are presented in three categories: clinical syndromes, personality dysfunctions, and medical complications.

CLINICAL SYNDROMES

Case Study: Shame

A powerful but often overlooked emotion associated with self-destructive behavior patterns is shame. As a matter of fact, it is rare for people in our society to use the term *shame*. Often, we use *guilt* or *embarrassment* when actually referring to shameful experiences. This tendency occurs despite research showing that shame is a very basic emotion that begins developing about age two; guilt arises around age eight.

More important than this distinction is the fact that guilt tends to be related to specific behaviors, while shame is associated with more general feelings about oneself. In other words, shame has more direct and broader impact on our self-esteem and tends to make us want to hide or run away from situations that bring us this emotion. By escaping or avoiding these situations, the shame-ridden person temporarily feels less defective and inferior.

Guilt, on the other hand, tends to be more situation specific—that is, a particular behavior or set of behaviors causes this emotion. As a consequence, guilt is less likely to cause us to "throw the baby out with the bathwater" in terms of our self-esteem. Moreover, when feeling guilty, we can often smooth things over with apologies, restitution, compensatory acts, or asking for forgiveness. Thus, there are more ways to cope with guilt to reduce internal stress and preserve the self-concept.

Because shame develops before guilt, the former can have a greater impact on us during childhood. For instance, the three-year-old who is continuously made to feel shameful about his or her body will feel ashamed before being able to appreciate fully what the emotion really means or to understand how inappropriate it is to be treated in this fashion. By the time this child grows into late childhood and adolescence, he or she has "bought into," or accepted, shame as a fundamental part of life that is inevitable.

Let's consider the case of Jane, a young woman we saw during her fifth psychiatric hospitalization. She was married with children and had tried to live a "normal" life. Although she showed periods of relative normalcy to the outside world, she was well aware that she was acting to cover up inner turmoil.

During childhood, Jane was sexually abused by a relative over a period of several years. While growing up, she avoided telling other family members about it, and she never had a close friend in whom to confide, so she told no one about the abusive episodes. She didn't believe that anyone who knew the truth could truly accept her as a person. Jane was caught between the proverbial rock and hard place: she needed to confide in someone, but feared doing so would result in shame and rejection.

Jane's grades in high school were quite poor. She also became involved with an abusive boyfriend. After high school, she married and had children. She was a working mom, but eventually lost her job because of inappropriate behavior at work. Her problems mounted at home, and more than once she made an attempt to kill herself. These attempts were mostly suicidal gestures that appeared to be cries for help.

Through many years of suffering, the main unshakable symptom Jane felt was shame. She hid her past from everyone, refusing to confide in her family, her husband, and even mental health workers at previous psychiatric facilities. Her reluctance seems hard to understand, but from her point of view, speaking about her shameful past would have brought on more shame—and shame was precisely what she had been running from all her life. Shame was a vital threat to her already low self-esteem. Many of her behaviors were negative and self-defeating, but they were consistent with her low self-esteem and intense feelings of shame.

Jane eventually sought professional help, and was psychiatrically hospitalized. In the hospital, she had few places to hide. The treatment and living circumstances placed her with people 24/7. It was difficult for her to keep her defenses up continuously. Moreover, she was faced with the reality of her suicide attempt and how it could affect her children and husband.

Gradually, Jane opened up in group therapy, where it was acceptable to self-disclose. Everyone was talking about their innermost feelings and conflicts. When the time seemed right, the therapist challenged her with the notion of subtle suicide. He said it seemed like she had been ambivalent about living for many years and wondered what would make a physically healthy mother with a supportive husband continue to feel that way. As she reviewed her history of social isolation and self-defeating and self-destructive acts, she came closer to revealing the truth. Becoming aware of her existence in the subtle suicide zone, as well as how she got there, helped her see a way out of her turmoil into a new life full of exciting possibilities. She saw a path to psychological freedom from her internal hell.

Finally, in an emotional display, one day in therapy she blurted out the truth about the sexual abuse and an abortion. To her surprise, the group accepted her. Shortly thereafter, she disclosed her secrets to her husband and family members, who showed understanding and compassion. Jane had released a tremendous personal burden, and she was no longer continuously ambivalent about living. She finally understood clearly the links between her adult behavior and the past. She became less preoccupied with herself and started listening to and helping others more. Her self-esteem increased and her shame decreased. Jane started becoming more intimate with others and set a goal to develop friends for the first time in her life. She knew her recovery was far from complete. She understood

40   Subtle Suicide

that she needed to reinforce the gains she made during outpatient therapy
and to continue to work on many other aspects of her life that either
needed repair or enhanced development. But once she stopped avoiding
the reality of the abusive events, and once she realized her shame was
unfounded and that her significant others would not reject her, she was
well on the road out of the subtle suicide zone.

Case Study: Shame Sprinkled with Guilt

It is rare for someone to experience a single emotion when engaging in
a behavioral pattern such as subtle suicide. This particular case study illustrates the concept of shame-infused guilt used by June Tangney. Guilt
becomes excessively destructive when it is linked with shame. The individual travels mentally from "Look at the terrible thing I did" to "I must be a
terrible person." In this case, negative feelings toward oneself became generalized beyond a specific guilt-inducing behavior.

Bonnie is a middle-aged woman who was hospitalized psychiatrically
on numerous occasions. Interestingly, she showed pretty much the same
patterns during each hospitalization. She would come in very demoralized
and depressed, and leave feeling somewhat better but still with flat emotion and little to say. Most of the time, her head remained down as she
spoke, avoiding eye contact. She had not been able to keep a full-time job
even though she had a college education, and she showed little, if any,
hope for the future.

Bonnie's family maintained a supportive stance. Psychiatric medications
seemed to give her little therapeutic benefit, which is not unusual for
subtle suicide sufferers. Prior to her most recent hospitalization, treatment
had focused mostly on her current life situation and psychiatric medications. This type of treatment, however, generally yields only temporary
relief from serious symptoms associated with subtle suicide.

A new therapist, therefore, took a different approach. Bonnie was reluc-
tant to offer much about her past, so the therapist carefully and slowly
guided her to a deeper exploration of what she was avoiding. Eventually,
with intense emotionality, Bonnie described an accident she had had many
years earlier. The accident led to the deaths of others and put Bonnie in
the hospital in a coma. When she finally came out of the coma, she had
no memory of the accident, but was sent to jail because there was evidence
she was to blame.

Bonnie rarely spoke about the accident and failed to see how much guilt
she carried over it. Furthermore, she did not understand that she now
believed she didn't deserve to live and enjoy life because her actions had
caused the death of others. For her, the guilt was absolute and unchange-
able. Nothing about her reaction to the accident could ever be changed.
Her approach to guilt was most unfortunate, because when an event leads

to guilt and the victim sees little hope for change, serious consequences result and are difficult to resolve. Bonnie's perception of her guilt left her unwilling to consider more appropriate ways to cope with the guilt or even to try to "turn over a new leaf." It was nearly impossible for her to realize that, while she could not change the past, it was within her direct control to become a better person in other important ways.

One reason Bonnie's guilt was difficult to resolve was that she lacked specific memories of the accident. Thus, she experienced a very vague sense of guilt that was hard to clarify and discuss. Nevertheless, in therapy she slowly realized that she had been very self-defeating and self-destructive for many years. She identified strongly with the possibility of subtle suicide and agreed that she had demonstrated a lifestyle consistent with this process for more than two decades. These insights were significant breakthroughs for Bonnie.

As she saw the connection between her long-term guilt, shame, and depression, the motivation to stop punishing herself increased. She acknowledged that it was time to accept what had happened and move on with her family life in more productive ways. As her mood and behavior became more positive, she received much more favorable feedback from others, which rewarded her for the constructive changes she was making. Hospital workers commented that she had shown incredible changes during her most recent hospitalization. Her outlook brightened, she voiced optimistic and hopeful attitudes, and she even made eye contact with others when talking.

By facing the guilt over the accident, Bonnie managed to reduce her shame about the event. Her negative emotional states had always been associated with social withdrawal, depression, and low-esteem. By lowering these emotions, she was able to become more sociable, hopeful, and constructive in her behaviors. The underlying causes of Bonnie's subtle suicide patterns were effectively weakened. Finally, she could reverse the domino effect that strangled her life and begin building positive momentum that could point her life in a better direction. She also learned that she needed to forgive herself—which is the focus of our next case study.

Case Study: Self-forgiveness

Forgiveness is an emotional experience closely related to guilt and shame. Psychological research on forgiveness emphasizes the benefits of accepting forgiveness from others, but doesn't tell us much about the harmful effects of not forgiving ourselves. Studies have shown how the compassion of being pardoned or forgiven "releases" the transgressor from much of the emotional burden brought on by an event. What happens, however, when the sufferer can't accept *self*-forgiveness? What lingering effects might occur? How might the situation be remedied? Jim's case touches on some of these questions.

When he came to our attention, Jim was an elderly man whose psychological functioning had deteriorated significantly in recent years. He had always been a somewhat obsessive and anxious man, but he became increasingly hopeless and depressed in his later years. In fact, he required psychiatric hospitalization for suicidal thinking and threats. These tendencies were shocking to his wife and adult child, because he was in good health and his previous life history was unremarkable in terms of significant psychological problems. Also, he had a supportive family and no financial problems.

Jim had been psychiatrically hospitalized previously, and he followed up with outpatient treatments for monitoring of several psychiatric medications. Nevertheless, his agitated depression persisted. He experienced little pleasure in life and showed minimal interest in doing anything for himself. He had low energy and frequently entertained thoughts of suicide as a way of ending his painful existence. In short, he did not feel life was worthwhile and could not see how his life would change. Jim fit the profile of a subtle suicide victim. As frequently is the case, even though filled with despair, he hung onto his miserable life because he still possessed some desire to live, as well as a need to avoid devastating his family by committing suicide.

Questioning Jim after his second hospitalization provided some interesting information. He reported recently becoming much more depressed after seeing a World War II documentary. He thought obsessively about this program and had little control over the constant upsetting and intrusive thoughts he had after seeing it. It turned out that these thoughts and feelings provided the keys to unlocking some causes behind his problems.

In therapy, Jim described how his best friend was with him during one of the longest and bloodiest battles of World War II. He and his friend watched many comrades get injured and die. They were honest about their survival chances, which appeared slim to them at the time. His friend asked if he would promise to look up his wife and child if he didn't make it. Jim, of course, responded with a definitive yes. Tragically, not long after their pact, his friend was killed in battle.

After returning home, Jim gradually became involved in an active and productive life. The last thing he wanted to do was think about the war and related atrocities. Unfortunately, he was unaware of the power of the unfinished "psychic business" lying beneath his consciousness. Like so many World War II veterans, he suffered from post-traumatic stress disorder (PTSD). This diagnosis was not yet available at that time, however, and treatment for soldiers with these symptoms was meager at best. Only the most serious of cases even received psychiatric or medical attention for being "shell shocked," a term used at the time. The main treatment methods were simply listening and giving support and rest to the victims. This approach appeared to help in many cases. Yet, there were thousands of unidentified sufferers who, like Jim, needed additional help to overcome their traumas but were left to fend for themselves.

Jim's PTSD was complicated by an additional and powerful reality: the unfulfilled promise to his best friend. For several decades, he was able to avoid thinking about or dealing with the guilt and shame associated with not following through on his promise, but the psychological baggage of the uncompleted pledge caught up to him as he got older. Like most of us, as Jim aged he found himself increasingly reviewing his life. As we age, more life stretches out behind us than in front of us, creating a tendency to look back and think more about our past. In addition, growing older gives us more time to think about the past, because we are less involved with work, raising children, and other responsibilities of young adulthood and middle age. Thus, unfinished business and unresolved emotional conflicts can become more powerful influences on psychological stability as we approach retirement and have a strong need to evaluate the level of integrity in our lives.

And so it was with Jim. The unfinished business of that pact with his wartime buddy became a heavier and heavier burden to bear. One might ask why he didn't simply pick up the phone and call his friend's survivors. This is a logical question, but it misses the point. Jim's reasons were driven not by logic but by emotions, something typical of so many people with self-defeating problems and subtle suicide actions. Jim was also doubly guilty: delaying the contact was one thing, but not even trying to make the contact was all the worse! Thus, wracked by guilt that had spread throughout his psyche like a metastasized cancer, he slowly descended into the subtle suicide zone.

Therapy with Jim focused on the development of his subtle suicide tendencies and lack of self-forgiveness. As he became aware of how PTSD helped immobilize him and cause him to avoid his friends, wife, and child, Jim's associated feelings of shame and guilt subsided. Although guilt and shame were involved in this case, lack of self-forgiveness appeared to be the central driving force to his subtly suicidal state. Usually, shame is heightened by the knowledge that others know about our perceived transgressions, but that was not the situation here. Jim was the only one who knew of his failure to deliver on his promise. As for guilt, Jim was able to reduce much of it by living a moral and wholesome life after returning home. Still, there was a part of Jim that couldn't shake the feeling that he didn't deserve to live. After all, he was fortunate enough to survive, but still couldn't muster the courage to make good on his promise. Perhaps, he thought, the better man had died during the war.

In therapy, Jim's self-analysis and self-confrontation proceeded along the following lines: He had lived a postwar life of integrity. He was an honorable, responsible man who had taken care of his family and was a trusted friend to many people. What else could he do? He couldn't change the past.

True, but he could reconstruct, change, and modify his thoughts about his past behavior. He did so; he forgave himself. The result was that his mood brightened, his energy increased, and his plans for the future returned. Nevertheless, he needed to remain in outpatient counseling to help maintain and strengthen his newly found positive perspectives and guard against a return of the guilt over his broken pledge.

Case Study: Parental Psychological Abuse

Psychological abuse by a parent is a major cause of psychopathology. Frequently, this type of upbringing causes disorders of mood, mainly depression and anxiety, as well as some form of personality disorder. Some affected individuals suffer beyond these disorders and develop subtle suicide as a result of this risk factor.

Consider Robert, who grew up in what from outward appearances was a traditional, conventional family. His father worked long hours to provide for the family and his mother took care of the children and home. However, there was an ever-present source of psychological pain in this family: his mom! Dad was far from a saint; Robert said his father could erupt into tirades when provoked and frustrated. However, most of his outbursts resulted from his wife's provocations. She was clearly a critical, demanding, and verbally abusive person. Most of the time, whatever family members did or didn't do was simply not good enough for her. No matter how hard they worked, she demeaned their efforts and achievements.

Growing up, Robert identified and modeled his behavior after his dad. However, even though he harbored a great deal of anger toward his mother, Robert paradoxically found himself drawn toward women like her as he grew older. He was accustomed to her type of treatment and, quite frankly, wouldn't have known what to do with an accepting, supportive, loving woman. Even though his mom's behavior was difficult to cope with, there was a comfort level with her predictability. This "security with the familiar" led him into a marriage and family life much like his own childhood. Like so many of the cases of subtle suicide that we review, he succeeded in recreating his past life, which gave him a sense of security but also awakened previous conflicts that were never resolved.

After establishing a somewhat successful career and having children, Robert's marriage predictably dissolved. He and his wife were, of course, both responsible for their poor marriage and divorce. For his part, Robert did not truly realize his marriage was a continuation of his battles with his mother. He did not understand how much of his anger toward his mom was misdirected onto his wife.

After the marriage broke up, Robert moved. For the first time, however, he moved a considerable distance from his parents. After the breakup, he also began outpatient treatment for anxiety and depression and continued with his profession. He stabilized somewhat and improved his psychological functioning for several years. Then, some major developments caused him to deteriorate significantly. First, he moved back to the area where his parents and grown children resided, a decision he regrets to this day. Second, his dad committed suicide shortly after a major argument with Robert. Third, he got involved in a mutually abusive relationship with a girlfriend. Finally, he began to abuse alcohol.

Robert was entering the subtle suicide zone. Although he started seeing a psychiatrist and was heavily medicated with psychotropic drugs, he continued to drink to the point of passing out. The rage he directed at his girlfriend, and her psychological abuse of him in return, did not make him feel better about himself, even after the relationship ended. He continued to have a vague sense of guilt about his father's death, and he was enraged and bitter toward his mom. He seemed incapable of an intimate relationship with a woman, but was quite lonely.

All this time, Robert was smoking heavily, and he told his therapist he didn't care if he died from the cigarettes. He knew the potential for lung cancer and other smoking-related dangers. He was also well aware of his own loss of lung capacity. Yet, he continued to smoke. Interestingly, he also continued with therapy.

These conflicting actions show Robert's ambivalence toward living: he wanted to live, but a part of him wanted to die. Why would someone who feels "It would be fine with me if I develop lung cancer and die" continue to engage in therapy and try to improve? That question strikes at the very heart of the subtle suicide process. At some level, the sufferer wants to continue living and come to grips with issues and conflicts. On the other hand, there is a strong avoidance of worthwhile life events and a fatalistic "So what if I die?" attitude. In Robert's case, which is not unusual, there was also intense guilt, shame, and self-directed anger. Robert desperately wanted to avoid hurting his kids with overt suicide the way his dad had hurt him. Still, there was a large part of him that felt too much pain to go on. Dying of smoking, of course, would not hurt others the way overt suicide would, or so he thought. Robert was trapped in a vicious downward spiral of self-defeating and self-destructive thoughts and actions that are the foundations of the subtle suicide zone.

Ultimately, Robert found some support and solace by attending regular meetings of Alcoholics Anonymous. Once alcohol was purged from his system, his psychiatric medications helped make his anxiety and depression more manageable so he could confront them. He had mixed reactions when his mother died. He suffered grief, of course, but was also somewhat relieved at putting to rest the source of some disturbing memories of his childhood. He moved out of his house, which was near hers, into an apartment physically and psychologically far from the memories of the family home.

Unlike some subtle suicide patients, Robert was quick to admit to being somewhat aware of the underlying dynamics of his problems. In fact, he was very open to discussing them. Moving out of his house and away from the family home helped reduce his tendency to dwell negatively on his past life. He continued psychotherapy, psychiatric medications, and attendance at AA meetings. On the surface, it seemed he was trying everything possible to help himself cope constructively. But to those who knew him well, his self-destructive demons were never fully purged. Frankly, it was amazing he was still alive. He survived many "blackouts" from consuming huge quantities of alcohol combined with his psychiatric medication. Beyond that, he didn't exercise and continued to smoke heavily. His behaviors continued to suggest he had desires both to live and to die. The alcohol and medications temporarily helped subdue his feelings of rage and guilt, but he battled with the desire to kill himself from time to time.

Robert is now retired and lives alone. He has improved greatly but still battles with staying out of the subtle suicide zone. He no longer drinks alcohol and continues his AA support meetings. For the most part, he has also resolved guilt feelings with respect to his dad's death, and his anger toward his mom continues to subside. However, he now fights loneliness. He is much more aware of his incapacity to love a woman in a mature way, but is trying to get over this problem through continued counseling and a more determined effort to meet "appropriate" women. Should he succeed in this last hurdle, he is confident he will be able to exit the subtle suicide zone. A lifetime of avoidance patterns, however, can be hard to overcome.

Case Study: Emotional Deprivation

People who are emotionally deprived as children have some distinct disadvantages and often feel that they are inadequate and can never measure up to others' standards. On the other hand, early emotional deprivation may lead to attitudes of entitlement: "I deserve special treatment as an adult because I was emotionally damaged as a child." In either case, intimate relationships tend to suffer. Interestingly, unlike most people who are abused or neglected, emotionally deprived individuals tend to suffer silently because the causes of their pain are not as obvious or likely to be noticed by others. They don't understand that, left unattended, early emotional deprivation can make them vulnerable to depression, unhappiness, and dysfunctional relationships in adulthood. As we see so often, however, our victims choose to avoid issues—in this case, suffering in silence is the avoidance technique—rather than confront them.

Victims of early emotional deprivation tend to be "like dogs chasing their tails" for approval in relationships. Initially they blame themselves when things go wrong or aren't working, and they try to compromise or make adjustments to reduce conflict and get things on a smoother track. Their willingness to make concessions often causes friends and lovers to disrespect them and take them for granted.

Early emotional deprivation also causes one to be drawn to people who are emotionally unavailable, especially in early adulthood. After all, isn't this emotional distance what they are accustomed to? (We saw this in the previous case of Robert.) Thus, they tend to run from partners who are consistently warm, giving, nurturing, and loving. Supportive social signals are aversive because of the uncertainty those signals produce about how to behave. Warm and loving interactions make them feel uncomfortable and undeserving. These dynamics even extend to the workplace, where they tend to be tireless employees who work like dogs for approval. In intimate relationships, however, they reside in "no-man's land." Uncomfortable and uncertain, they run from healthy relationships, but ironically may continue to seek the entitlements they feel they deserve. This pattern, of course, is obviously self-defeating, and the person is at risk for becoming one of the living dead.

How do people get out of this downward spiral? Eventually, they need to find it intolerable to be treated like a child and be willing to act more maturely in their relationships. They must become aware of how emotional deprivation led to their difficulties and find the courage to change the thoughts and behaviors that maintain their unhappiness and dysfunctional relationships. They need to accept love from a significant other and make their primary need for true intimacy realistic and based on mutual sharing.

Mary fits this type of profile. She was initially diagnosed and treated for depression as a young adult. By the time she came to our attention, she had been treated for more than a decade, primarily by a psychiatrist. She had been psychiatrically hospitalized more than once and even submitted to electro-convulsive shock therapy (ECT), a treatment typically reserved for patients who have not responded sufficiently to psychiatric medication and psychotherapy. ECT is generally a last resort for those with significant depression and/or suicidal intentions or actions.

Although Mary originally began treatment as a young adult, she said her depression began much earlier. She could remember being mildly depressed during junior high and high school. This type of depression, called *dysthymia*, usually begins in childhood or adolescence, develops gradually, and is not obvious to others, even the sufferer. Dysthymia is a moderate but chronic form of depression. Unfortunately, untreated it leaves the depressed person more vulnerable to major depression. Dysthymics are like people standing on one foot. They can be more easily knocked down, into a major depression, by the blows of life than the nondepressed individual can.

For many reasons, dysthymics may go many years without formal treatment. They tend to have personality dynamics, such as heightened feelings of anxiety and guilt, that can make them avoid seeking help. They get accustomed to having low morale and seem able to function in underachieving ways, with or without being on psychiatric medication or in therapy. In other words, they can go through the motions of life without consistent and special attention to their condition.

Those who suffer from dysthmia are unaware of these dynamics because they have grown up this way. It takes them a long time to realize the way they relate to life isn't "normal." By the time they realize others enjoy life on a regular basis more than they do, it's too late to defend against becoming dysthymic because they already have the disorder. The die is cast and their depression has become well established.

Interestingly, we have found that dysthymics tend to respond minimally to antidepressants. This ineffectiveness of medication makes sense because the underlying causes of their depression have become a part of their personalities and their everyday way of life. Dysthymics develop patterns of thoughts and behaviors that keep them stuck in depression. They have well-learned tendencies for being pessimistic, self-defeating, underachieving, and self-blaming. Is it any wonder they don't respond in positive ways to psychiatric medications? We cannot expect medication to change personalities or life situations. Only sufferers can make these changes, which require a great deal of motivation and effort.

Unfortunately, most dysthymics don't appear on the therapy radar screen until they have experienced a serious adjustment problem or major depression. Even more unfortunately, if they rebound from these adjustment or major depression symptoms, the dysthymia is often left undiagnosed and untreated. After all, they have returned to their previous levels of functioning. What more is left to treat? They seem to be back to "normal."

Mary's case shows many of these dysthymic dynamics. She said she never felt she had a "father connection." "He saw us, but just went through the motions." To make matters worse, shortly after divorcing her mom during early childhood, Mary's dad married another woman who also had children. This situation made Mary feel even more emotionally distant from him. She described her mom as "the best" and respected her for "raising us on her own." Mom had put herself through school and then worked double shifts at her job to make ends meet. But as a result, Mary's mother generally wasn't available to give practical and emotional support. She simply didn't have much time or energy left for Mary and her siblings.

Mary graduated from college and entered a human services profession. She eventually married a man who was like her father—generally unavailable emotionally. (Again we see this ironic pattern we saw in earlier cases: Mary chose a man who continued the emotional frustrations and conflicts she had with her dad while growing up.) Mary took on a life path much like her mom's, with one major exception: she didn't have any children. Having a child, of course, would have rid her of some emotional deprivation, at least temporarily. Moreover, it would have given her a major distraction from her painful existence. She became pregnant, but unfortunately she miscarried, and her physician said she would probably never have her own biological child because of infertility problems. Her frustration and disappointment over this news were multiplied at work, where she had close interaction with infants.

The combination of Mary's predisposing risk factors from childhood and her miscarriage drove her into major depression with suicidal thoughts and intentions. She had never cared much about living. Now, her ambivalence about living became more intense. Whereas she used to think about suicide only occasionally, such thoughts were now a daily occurrence. She had entered the subtle suicide zone.

Mary made some actual suicide attempts over a two-year period. Part of her was still fighting to live, but other powerful forces within her were driving for avoidance of psychological pain and suicide. She agreed to psychiatric medications and ECT treatments. ECT, however, did little more than rob her of memories and make her feel more like a failure. Visits with a counselor were similarly unsuccessful because the treatments missed a major point: her deeply felt ambivalence about living interfered with the shock and other treatment efforts. She could not maintain efforts to change because her motivation to do so would come and go along with her wishes to die.

Mary had been on an extended leave of absence from work when she began psychotherapy with a new psychologist. The absence from work helped her focus on treatment, but also gave her a lot of time to think about her negative life circumstances. She had become more and more hopeless and depressed and increasingly negative about her marriage. She couldn't see herself going back to working with infants, but saw little hope of finding another position with equal pay and benefits. Her career was the one thing she had been proud of, and now even that source of strength had crumbled.

Initially, therapy focused primarily on instilling increased hope and analyzing Mary's ambivalence about living. Her therapist introduced her to the concept of subtle suicide. She had never heard of such a concept and was intrigued by it. Mary saw that she fit the general profile of subtle suicide sufferers and agreed the profile could be a starting point for the battle that lay ahead. She considered the possibility that her problem was not her suicidal thoughts or her periods of depression that standard treatments did not change but the self-defeating behaviors that she was performing virtually every day.

Mary understood she needed to want to live more than to avoid her problems by death. Her struggle was difficult, but gradually she started to change her characteristic self-defeating and self-sabotaging behaviors that were reducing her will to live. Rather than falling into the victim's role, she began thinking about how she might make her career and marriage better. She began to feel more hopeful and stopped resorting to thoughts of suicide as a way out of life's struggles. She saw that if she did not escape from the subtle suicide zone, she might not survive eventual overt suicide attempts. This reality had not scared her much before. But now, as she faced her ambivalence about living more honestly and constructively, her desire to live increased.

Throughout therapy, Mary remained on psychiatric medication prescribed by her psychiatrist. One suggestion from her psychologist was for her to see a different psychiatrist to get a fresh perspective. Her current psychiatrist was focusing on her medication and not on encouraging new behaviors. He told her she should wait for the drugs to "kick in," and then she would feel like behaving more productively. He was afraid to let her go back to work, but there was also a danger that she would wait too long to return to active employment. Her psychologist pointed out that she needed to feel productive again, and returning to work would help that process and give her less time for negative thinking.

Mary followed the recommendation to switch to a new psychiatrist, who reduced her psychiatric medications, which were essentially numbing her. Shortly thereafter, she made some significant behavior changes. She returned to work, but she took a different position. This was a lateral move, but importantly it gave her less direct involvement with infants, involvement that only reminded her of her infertility.

At home, she confronted her husband about her unmet wants and needs. Previously, Mary had been afraid to confront her husband because she felt undeserving of being treated better. Frankly, she had let him become an egocentric and entitled partner, increasing her feelings of emotional deprivation. This situation wasn't good 'for either of them, and she finally decided to confront these patterns in their relationship. Subsequently, he entered therapy with a different practitioner to address his own dysfunctions, with a hope the marriage would improve.

Mary was now ready to face her main risk factor, emotional deprivation. Until this time, her chronic approach to problems and conflicts was avoidance. Her anxiety about emotional deprivation, which began early in her life, fostered this avoidance pattern and led her to depression. Deep down, she had a life force that guided her will to live, but the avoidance patterns counteracted that positive force with: "What's the point? Could dying be that bad?" These are typical avoidance thoughts for someone in the subtle suicide zone, and these thoughts must be dealt with.

The subtly suicidal person must be encouraged to express new actions—behaviors that represent approaching life and not avoiding it. That is precisely what happened with Mary. She returned to work, confronted her husband, took a more active role in their relationship, stopped waiting for the psychiatric drugs to kick in, and performed actions that made her feel more worthwhile. With encouragement provided in counseling and newly discovered feelings of personal control, Mary began to lower her daily psychiatric drug dosages and to deal with her feelings of dependence on the medications. She developed the strength to face her primary adversary, fear of emotional deprivation. For instance, she decided that if her husband couldn't love her the way she needed, then she would live alone or find someone else who would.

At the time of this writing, the fate of Mary's marriage remains uncertain, although it has improved. She has become much more accepting of herself and her husband. They adopted a baby and have discovered more things they have in common and a greater purpose in life that they can share. Mary certainly has more reasons to live, and she now allows herself to be open to new and exciting possibilities for the future.

Case Study: Anxiety Disorder

Anxiety disorders are common and can be extremely debilitating. Unfortunately, many people also suffer from anxiety as a secondary part of some other psychological difficulty. This complication is particularly true in the case of depression, because people who are depressed also tend to have high anxiety levels and vice versa.

Individuals with strong anxiety obviously have difficulty relaxing and enjoying life. They avoid many situations that could lead to pleasure, achievement, and personal growth. Moreover, chronic anxiety robs them of their life energy and can create or worsen medical problems. Is it any wonder that unbridled anxiety can cause depression and diminish a will to live? When not addressed effectively and in a timely manner, people with significant chronic anxiety problems can easily drift into the subtle suicide zone. Not all people with chronic anxiety struggle with subtle suicide, though. An anxiety disorder can be a significant risk factor, but other factors usually must be present to move a person into the subtle suicide zone. These dynamics are reflected well in the case of Greg, who suffered from obsessive-compulsive disorder (OCD), a particularly difficult type of anxiety disorder to treat.

During childhood and adolescence, Greg was the altar-boy type: he was polite, respectful, and generally stayed out of trouble. He was raised a strict Catholic and attended parochial school. He took teachings by nuns and other pastoral figures very seriously, including the notion that God knows our every thought, and that thoughts can be sinful. As an adult in therapy, Greg remembered that when he was a teenager he was extremely self-conscious and guilty about his adolescent thoughts and urges. This guilt over lustful thoughts and impulses continued into young adulthood. These were initial indications of unresolved underlying issues that would come back to haunt Greg. Unfortunately, during adolescence and young adulthood he avoided facing his guilt and didn't seek any form of counseling.

After graduating from high school and enrolling in college, Greg decided to enter a seminary. While there, his obsessive thinking about sexual anxiety and guilt increased. He found himself constantly confessing sinful thoughts and impulses that most young men accept as natural and normal. He left the seminary shortly after one of the priests asked him to show him his penis and he complied because of his submissive and obedient personality, even though this act increased his self-doubts, anxiety, and feelings of shame.

Looking back, it is clear that a developing anxiety disorder was putting Greg at great risk for serious problems. He also showed vulnerability to intense feelings of shame and guilt. He did everything possible to avoid these uncomfortable emotions, but such denial is generally a waste of time. Tormented by uncontrollable thoughts, all he could manage to do was control his behaviors. To our knowledge, he has never committed any immoral or illegal act.

Despite struggling with high levels of anxiety during most of his adulthood, Greg managed to marry, raise children, and have a reasonably successful career. Nevertheless, there were significant bumps in his road. His marriage ended in divorce. Along the way, he became estranged from one of his children, who developed a coalition against him with his ex-wife. Still, he muddled along until he retired.

After retirement, Greg had little to do except play golf. His children were pretty much on their own, and he remained alienated from his wife and one adult child. He had far too much time to think about his failures, transgressions, and regrets, and he became his own worst enemy. He mentally pounded himself with anxiety and guilt, even though by any objective standard he had lived a very moral and productive life.

In an attempt to avoid negative thoughts and feelings, Greg developed extreme OCD symptoms. Every aspect of his day had to be rigidly ordered and structured; every action needed careful planning and execution, with no room for flexibility. Only by maintaining vigilance and absolute control over his schedule could he avoid the demons deep in his mind.

As is generally the case, his protective OCD behaviors were only partially successful, and Greg slowly lost his will to live. When he felt that he could no longer endure the pain inside him, he overdosed on psychiatric medications and was in a coma for more than a month. Miraculously, he survived. He then saw two different psychiatrists and a psychologist. The psychiatrists prescribed numerous psychiatric medications. He also submitted to ECT and was admitted to several psychiatric institutions over a period of months. Greg's condition was so severe that he was treated at a clinic specializing in behavioral treatment of OCD and was hospitalized for almost a year at a long-term psychiatric care facility. Around this time, he began psychotherapy with a new psychologist.

Greg demonstrated a major symptom of subtle suicide: ambivalence about living. On the positive side, he lived in a group home where he could receive therapeutic support and avoid being alone most of the time. He also visited regularly with two of his children, but had little contact with friends and still did not speak with his other child. At the same time, he smoked excessively and openly admitted to a desire to die from lung cancer or some other smoking-related medical condition. When confronted with the possibility that he fit the subtle suicide profile, he agreed, but was still unwilling to change his smoking behavior or work on finding more desire to live. He only agreed to concentrate on the OCD symptoms that caused him such great distress (over a long period of treatment, these symptoms subsided significantly).

Eventually, Greg was helped by a few major events in his life. His ex-wife died and he was able to reconcile with his estranged child. This process brought the entire family, which by now included grandchildren, closer together. Then he was diagnosed with cancer. The family rallied around him. The reality of the cancer diagnosis confronted him with a decision about whether he really wanted to live or continued to desire death, wasting his life with self-destructive thoughts and actions. Ultimately, he decided to put an end to the subtle suicide, and he quit smoking. Although his OCD symptoms remained, he made some progress in this area, as well, and forced himself to live day to day without being dominated by the need for order and predictability.

Greg became more involved in daily activities with his children and grandchildren. He began to see how he would "live on" in his grandchildren. As a result, not only did his life became more tolerable but he was also relieved of his ambivalence about living. His positive activities in approaching life meant he spent less time and energy on thinking about dying. With help, he taught himself to approach life and to continue challenging his OCD condition.

The unfortunate part of this case, of course, is how long Greg delayed facing his innermost conflicts. Stricken with guilt and anxiety from his childhood, he let those emotions rule him and did not make the most of his adult years. He is a remarkable example of how one can "live" in the subtle suicide zone for a long time. The ultimate irony for Greg is that he came to grips with his subtle suicide condition only after developing cancer; he decided to live a more productive life only after being given a virtual medical death sentence.

Case Study: More than Chronic Pain

Cases of chronic pain seem to be increasing at an alarming rate. It seems we all know someone who suffers from almost continuous pain due to some medical condition or accident. Often these individuals are unable to work and suffer a significant loss of income. These sufferers frequently have to fight insurance or disability carriers for many years, especially after an auto or work-related accident.

Severe pain helps cause frustration, anxiety, depression, and other negative emotions that impact on the sufferer as well as significant others.

More time spent at home can create negative circumstances for everyone, and there is often the need for major role changes in all of the family members. Career-oriented individuals may suddenly find themselves at home, while their partner goes to work to maintain family income. Also, psychiatric medication side effects or drug abuse/dependence issues may cause yet another layer of destructive elements for the sufferer.

Such situations, which can happen to anyone at any time, can leave the chronic pain patient with little will to live. Some sufferers enter the subtle suicide zone, others do not. The reasons for this discrepancy are varied and complex. For example, some people have stronger support systems or are able to continue working. These factors help boost hope and constructive coping styles. Others, however, have predisposing risks, such as a history of significant depression or anxiety, alcoholism, drug abuse, or other medical problems. The case that follows highlights many of these issues.

When he came in for therapy, George was in his thirties and single, had a full-time job, and was going to school part-time to earn a college degree. He was obese and suffering from major depression. He was awkward in social situations with strangers and tended to be emotionally dependent, especially with his parents. In a sense, he had never "cut the cord" when it came to his parents, and they watched over him like he was a teenager. He had been diagnosed with insulin-dependent diabetes and had several herniated discs, although he was not suffering from chronic pain. He was being treated psychiatrically with antidepressants and anti-anxiety medications.

Over the next six years or so, George had four accidents, which increased his medical and pain difficulties. Three of the accidents (none his fault) were auto related. The other, oddly enough, was caused by a malfunction of an elevator. Although none of these accidents could be characterized as serious, his injured discs and obesity made his existing medical problems and pain much worse. Although he had dealt successfully with a prior bout of major depression, new psychological problems loomed on the horizon. With each accident, he lost more mobility and had to cope with more neck and back pain. Visits with doctors and medical testing became routine, as did appointments with lawyers. Eventually, he resigned his job because he could no longer perform his duties adequately. During therapy sessions, he began to say things like, "Sometimes I feel death would be a blessing," "I have no goals or motivation," and "How much can a person take?"

As George drifted into the subtle suicide zone, he began to show reckless and self-destructive behavior patterns. He spent money foolishly, gambled, ate excessively, engaged in sexually promiscuous behavior, and took poor care of his diabetes. Although there was a part of him that wanted to live, that part was fading fast. Pain medications gave only partial relief, and none of the many specialists he met with recommended surgery for his significant back and neck problems. He was faced with the likelihood of a lifetime of disability, and he wasn't even forty years old. To make matters worse, his dad died the day before his fourth and final accident as George was driving to the hospital to see him.

To his credit, George continued therapy for more than seven years. This commitment helped him face his self-destructive behavior patterns and cope more effectively with what was assuredly a very unusual and torturous situation. His psychological state gradually shifted from major depression to a milder but more chronic form of depression, dysthymia, which we saw earlier in Mary's case. Additionally, he became focused on his bodily functioning, which is both common and understandable in a case like his. The only time he was free of pain was when he lay in bed. As a result, he was socially withdrawn and much less active than before the accidents. Nevertheless, he continued to go to school part-time.

It took several years of counseling, but eventually George was able to lose weight and monitor his diabetes better. Additionally, he brought his spending, gambling, and promiscuous sexual behavior under control. The bottom line is that he faced his subtle suicide dilemma and decided to leave this zone behind. He finally learned to confront his dependency on his parents and others. Certainly, it helped that he was almost guaranteed a very large personal injury settlement from one of the accidents, which gave him additional hope that he could independently finance a return to college and a career change.

When George finally completed his college course work, he found a better job. He began to feel more productive and more confident socially. He felt there was finally some purpose to his life. He focused more on his future, and physical pain bothered him less. Although he couldn't say his hope for the future was great, he did comment, "If the old me was still around, I wouldn't be."

He survived long enough to let another factor help him: ironically, his father's death. George witnessed the powerful and negative impact his dad's death had upon his mom and extended family. This impact provided a lasting memory that motivated him to avoid hurting his family members in a similar fashion. His increased will to live helped him immeasurably with his self-destructive tendencies. Eventually he finished a college degree and obtained a professional job. He says that his chronic pain is much more tolerable when he is working, because his mind is distracted.

Case Study: Post-Traumatic Stress Disorder

PTSD symptoms occur after one has undergone some traumatic experience. Common experiences include rape, horrendous accidents, warfare, and other death-related events. PTSD victims may have watched someone else die (or almost die) or faced a death-threatening experience. However, we are increasingly aware that other types of experiences can also cause

PTSD, such as loss of an important job, seeing a spouse or lover cheat, or facing the reality of having to serve a jail term. Whatever the case, PTSD is an anxiety disorder that often coexists with other psychological disorders, such as depression and personality dysfunctions. Typical symptoms of PTSD include sleep disturbances, nightmares, panic and anxiety attacks, social withdrawal, and extreme avoidance of anything resembling the original traumatic event.

This case concerns Jennifer, who experienced significant PTSD, along with major depression and personality dysfunctions, most notably borderline and dependent personality styles. This diagnosis came from both clinical impressions and psychological testing data.

The primary precipitating factor that originally drove Jennifer to a psychiatrist was being forced to resign her job. She had worked hard to establish herself in her chosen profession. Unfortunately, some indiscretions at work put her in legal jeopardy. Her employer told her the company would not pursue charges if she resigned. By doing so, she avoided public scrutiny and possible legal entanglements. However, she lost a position that was a pivotal part of her life and self-image. Moreover, she felt great shame and embarrassment among her friends and other people who knew what happened. As a result, she experienced a lot of social anxiety and massive social withdrawal, both of which compounded her problems.

These traumatic events were severe enough to cause an outbreak of PTSD symptoms and eventual psychiatric hospitalization. Jennifer was treated with psychiatric medication for more than a decade. During this time, she did not receive intensive psychotherapy or diagnostic psychological assessment to help design appropriate treatment strategies.

When Jennifer finally found her way to psychological counseling through the advice of a friend, she was middle-aged, married with children, and unemployed and weighed more than three hundred pounds. She was "maxed out" on a cocktail of five psychiatric medications for depression, anxiety, bipolar disorder, and OCD. She was receiving a "shotgun" approach to psychiatric medical treatment—try them all and something is bound to "hit." When asked about therapeutic goals, she could not say much except that she hoped the medications would make her feel better. But all they did was "numb" her to life, help her gain 120 pounds, and sap her energy and spirit. Essentially, the psychiatric medications kept her in a zombie-like state, "helping" her escape certain realities she would eventually have to confront and accept.

During therapy, Jennifer provided information about her early childhood. She described her father as overly attached and permissive. She never knew her mother, who died shortly after giving birth to Jennifer. Jennifer was unsure of the actual cause of the mom's death because it was "hush-hush" in the family. Nevertheless, she admitted to some vague feelings of guilt over this loss. After the mother's death, her father, older siblings, and two aunts raised her. She described the aunts as "paranoid, manipulative, and perfectionistic."

As we noted earlier, Jennifer's adult problems began when she was forced to resign from her job. Soon afterward, she became suicidal and was hospitalized. During her hospitalization, she was diagnosed with major depression, but with neither PTSD nor a personality disorder. She said she was never diagnosed or treated for anything other than major depression, bipolar disorder, and OCD. Apparently, during her long period of treatment, there was a lot of confusion concerning her diagnoses.

For ten years, Jennifer basically did nothing constructive with her life. She took psychiatric medications as prescribed, because they validated her psychiatric disability and justified her lack of purposeful activity. At the same time, the medications gave her a "whatever" attitude toward life. She didn't care about her physical appearance or health. She had a ready-made excuse for not working, cooking, housecleaning, or exercising. She didn't care much about anything, including whether she lived or died. Jennifer didn't care about making progress with her psychiatrist, either. In fact, she worried that showing significant improvement might lead to loss of her disability benefits, which helped support her family. If she died of a heart attack, that would be fine with her. Death would release her from the psychological hell that was her existence. Jennifer had joined the living dead.

Jennifer was socially isolated and watched her husband work about sixty hours per week to make ends meet. She felt badly about herself. Not only was she ashamed over the loss of her job, she was also ashamed that her husband had to work so many hours. She continued to be haunted by the loss of her job and avoided being seen in the community as much as possible. She felt she did not deserve to be happy, a feeling that was not a new one for Jennifer because, deep down, she associated her birth with her mother's death. The more recent job problems simply reinforced her belief that she was not entitled to a good life. Her outward behavior, however, gave little indication of her internal turmoil. Outwardly, she appeared to be a lazy woman with no ambition who wanted her husband, the government, or whomever to take care of her.

What others couldn't see was the depth of Jennifer's depression and trauma. She was a fractured person who was in the subtle suicide zone for well over a decade. She engaged in some secretive, impulsive behavior patterns that, if discovered by others, could traumatize her more severely and have a negative impact on others. She engaged in these self-defeating and self-destructive behaviors for years with full knowledge of their potential consequences, but showed little concern over being caught. During this time period, she also survived a bout with cancer. When asked about how she related to the cancer issue, she said it really didn't scare her; she didn't care whether she made it through and lived or not.

Progress in therapy took more than a year. Thorough psychological assessment and analysis of pertinent background information led to a diagnosis of dysthymia, PTSD, and dependent personality. Also, Jennifer was referred to a different psychiatrist for a second opinion and possible changes in her psychiatric medication regimen. This referral led to significant reductions in her medication. Finally, her psychologist described her as fitting the subtle suicide profile and discussed the likely conditions causing this condition.

She agreed with the subtle suicide analysis, and gradually showed improvement during therapy. She began to lose weight, ended her impulsive acting-out behaviors, and became more active in taking better care of herself and the household. She started feeling better and more in control of her life. As expected, reducing the psychiatric medications gave her more energy but also increased her anxiety. She was no longer numb to life. She was experiencing the lows and highs that are natural and expected parts of living. Therefore, she needed to be helped to channel her renewed energy into constructive pursuits. This process wasn't easy, but she needed to give herself reasons to live and to exit the subtle suicide zone where she would be vulnerable to further problems.

When Jennifer acknowledged that she was in the subtle suicide zone, she cleared the first hurdle in the recovery process: she accepted and faced her vulnerabilities. She was, for instance, only a step away from becoming overtly suicidal. Also, her diabetes and obesity made her vulnerable to many serious medical problems that, if they didn't kill her, would certainly make her life less worth living. Once she accepted her condition, she found it easier to begin exercising, walking, and managing food intake. She also became more involved in managing the household and stopped hanging around with people who had proved to be a bad influence on her.

In general, Jennifer was able to accept and recognize her past regrets and move on with her life in a more positive fashion. This acceptance process allowed her to put more energy into things she could control in her present. The fact that she enacted these changes made it clear that she was motivated to leave the subtle suicide zone. Her life force began to become dominant over her death impulse. Reductions in her medications, which previously had only dulled her ambition and energy, along with corresponding therapy strategies that helped her gain more control over her actions and her thinking, put her on the road to recovery.

Case Study: Rejection Turned Inward

We have all experienced rejection, and we know how it hurts and angers us. What most of us haven't experienced is *chronic* rejection. An ongoing pattern of rejection can lead to reactions as extreme as the killings we have seen at schools, post offices, and government buildings.

Children who are targets of teasing and aggression are at greater risk for depression and lower in self-esteem than kids who are not such targets. Depressed children also tend to demonstrate poor social skills. Therefore, we can argue that depression in children may be caused, at least in part, by problems in interacting with others and learning how to solve conflicts and disagreements. Poor social skills seem to foster peer rejection, which leads to lower self-esteem and more depression. A vicious cycle may develop when the depressed child becomes less socially competent over time, leading to even more intense social difficulties. Thus, seeds for serious problems in social development can be peer related and may begin early in childhood.

The case that follows shows how peer rejection can help cause subtle suicide. Once again, however, we see that other factors can combine to create a baffling and seemingly unpredictable result. Realistically, it appears that some lessons can only be learned in retrospect, especially when dealing with complex phenomena like subtle suicide.

Danny, a young man in outpatient treatment, was struggling with college issues, his social life, and mood regulation. He was the youngest of several siblings, from an intact and supportive family. His immediate family had no psychiatric history, and his brothers and sisters were functioning well. His parents cooperated in providing relevant historical information to help develop treatment strategies. Danny, however, provided little information. In therapy, he acted defensively, as if he didn't really have any serious problems. He tried to make a joke out of most attempts to get him to self-disclose. He was generally compliant with treatment efforts, although mostly in a passive and uninterested "Okay, doc, anything you say" manner. However, he was adamantly opposed to psychiatric medication.

Danny had had one psychiatric hospitalization many years earlier. His parents were now sorry they hadn't done everything possible to prevent the hospitalization. The main effects of his brief treatment were that it made him dislike and resist taking his psychiatric medication, lowered his self-esteem, and increased his feelings of shame. He also had some previous contact with school counselors and a psychologist. The latter suggested he had bipolar disorder. A brief stint on a psychiatric mood stabilizer medication seemed to work, but he did not want to be stigmatized as a "mental patient," so he stopped taking the drug.

Because his siblings were much older, Danny lived like an only child who had several surrogate parents. His brothers and sisters did well in school and showed mostly relaxed, laid-back temperaments. Danny, on the other hand, although intelligent, was high-strung and had considerable social skills deficits. Thus, when the family moved from a large urban area to a more rural one, he had a lot of trouble making friends and getting along with peers, especially boys. It wasn't unusual for him to come home from school in tears with bruises, cuts, and scratches. When his parents asked what happened, almost always he refused to discuss it.

Danny's parents repeatedly tried to get to the bottom of his problems but to no avail. At school, he was treated like an outsider who had come from the Big City. He lived about five miles from the elementary school, which isolated him from schoolmates. Also, his family had a higher income level than most of his peers. These factors made it harder for Danny to become friends with the kids at school. Thus, he was by himself at school much of the time and became a ready-made target for teasing and bullying.

Despite Danny's social difficulties, he managed to do well academically, and eventually he went to a nearby private school for junior high and high school. His social problems, of course, followed him. By this time, his dad had retired and his siblings were adults. He continued to yearn for a circle of friends to call his own, but he had trouble making friends at the new school because he had not developed good social skills when younger. He got along fairly well with girls, but kept on having problems with boys. He continued to perform well academically but began to show serious mood swings, and much of the time he was irritable and angry.

His problems escalated when he went to college. Although he lived an easy drive from home, his parents felt he would benefit from living in the dorm at college. Not surprisingly, Danny did not adjust well at college and once again did not make solid friends. Even though he lived at school, he tended to drift back to his old neighborhoods when he could. He would hang out with younger high school kids, who quickly learned to take advantage of him on a regular basis. They damaged his car, beat him up, and stole from him. Still, in self-defeating fashion, he kept hanging out with them even though they constantly mistreated him. He finally broke away, but only after some problems with the police developed and he realized he would end up in jail if he continued to associate with this group.

Danny's avoidance patterns continued. He transferred to a different college and lived at home. At this time, he also began psychotherapy for the first time as an adult. He worked part-time and had many acquaintances, especially females. He also got involved with another group of young men who were more abusive than the former ones. He spent thousands of dollars catering to their wishes in an effort to be friends with them. One of the men, the informal leader of the pack, was particularly manipulative and abusive. Once again, Danny kept trying to befriend these guys and hoped they would accept him, even though they used and abused him.

Few people knew what was really happening. Details surfaced only when his parents heard from the police and found some of his billing records. His credit card balance totaled over thirty thousand dollars from buying gifts, dinners, and other items for this new group of young men. Everyone now begged Danny to stay away from these guys, but he refused to do so. A lifetime of rejection from males, together with low self-esteem and shame, kept him embedded in a pool of self-defeat and self-destruction, and he desperately sought acceptance from those who used and rejected him. The futility of Danny's actions was painful for everyone to see.

It was hard to determine to what extent Danny was consuming alcohol and other substances, but it was clear that substance abuse was part of his life. Also, abuse from peers continued. For example, he had to go to the hospital one night because of a stab wound. He also had a brief stay in prison for a harassment-related offense. Things were definitely beginning to escalate out of control. Danny became accustomed to being treated like an abused animal. Although he was lonely and longed for friendship and companionship, he didn't know what to do with people who treated him well. He ran away from invitations from others who wanted to get to know him better. This is the ultimate irony: starving for acceptance, Danny avoided those who reached out to him and stayed with those who mistreated him.

Danny's feelings of hopelessness were growing exponentially. He saw a psychiatrist, but wouldn't take any psychiatric medicine other than an antidepressant. After he was on the antidepressant for several weeks, his mother noticed some changes in his mood. On the positive side, he opened up and joked around more. On the other hand, he had a faraway stare at times. She was concerned, but there were not enough indicators to set off a major alarm. Then, Danny began missing appointments with both the psychiatrist and psychologist. He gave no indication of why he missed these sessions, nor did he suggest any particular problem with continuing treatment.

Then there was yet another "incident" when his car was damaged by so-called friends. Few other details came to light, but his parents figured out that his car had been stolen and he was roughed up and robbed. This was the last straw, even for Danny! After years of being a victim of bullying, he confronted the ringleader of the group. Although the details are somewhat ambiguous, he shot and killed both the ringleader "friend" and himself. These events proved to be the tragic ending to his life of great potential, never to be fulfilled. Obviously, there were no winners here.

Danny's parents remain convinced that the antidepressant medication somehow activated his capacity to be impulsively hostile toward himself and others. Initially, they were not convinced their son had been subtly suicidal for many years. Eventually, however, they were able to see how his self-defeating acts were part of a self-destructive orientation of "I don't care what others do to me or what happens to me." Danny let others repeatedly victimize him. He allowed himself to get into huge debt. Rejection by others seemed to fuel his desire to prove his worth to those who put him down. His actions suggested that he wanted peer acceptance, no matter what the cost.

We still ask, almost in disbelief, "Why did Danny put up with all of this misery for so long, only to eventually become so desperate?" The answer, of course, is complex, but psychologists know the crucial importance of healthy peer interactions when young. Danny was deprived of peer inter-actions during critical early developmental years. Healthy development requires peer interaction and acceptance.

Danny became so socially dysfunctional that he avoided interaction with nonabusive peers. He lived not only without acceptance but also with continued rejection and abuse from peers. In a sadly ironic way, his only "acceptance" could be found in those who abused and took advantage of him. His coping patterns had developed in a context of rejection from others, and he could function only in that context. Doing so, however, required an indifferent "Who cares?" approach to life. As that approach became stronger and stronger, he ventured deeper and deeper into the subtle suicide zone and became one of the living dead. He felt so shameful and had such low self-esteem that he was unable to cope constructively with his social issues. Establishing a healthy friendship with a peer who would not abuse him and take advantage of him was simply a foreign process. In Danny's own eyes, he was not worth such treatment; he felt he deserved harsh and abusive treatment from his acquaintances.

Danny did not escape the subtle suicide zone, which proved fatal in his case. His inability to be more self-disclosing with his parents and health-care professionals did not help them or him clarify his core psychological issues and subtle suicide condition. Thus, we see that subtle suicide patterns, when left untreated, may snowball into overt suicide and even homicide.

Case Study: Learning Disability

Alice is a middle-aged woman with a history of severe learning disabilities and attention deficit hyperactivity disorder (ADHD). She has also been psy-chiatrically hospitalized as an adult. The causes of her problems date back to early childhood. Consistent with research on ADHD, she showed many developmental and psychological problems, including deficits in motor coor-dination and social skills, anxiety, depression, learning disorders, opposi-tional and conduct problems, and marked parent–child conflicts.

Starting school was traumatic for Alice. She was hyperactive, but diag-nosis and treatment for ADHD were pretty much unheard-of when she was a child. She also showed extreme learning and motor disabilities, including dyslexia. The learning problems were so extensive that she is now functionally illiterate as an adult. Her limitations led to a lot of teas-ing and disapproval from peers during her early school years. She dreaded going to school, and quite frankly, her teachers were horrified at the pros-pect of spending an entire academic year with her. "I spent most of my time out in the hallway," Alice recalls.

Adding to these school problems, Alice's father drank heavily and used his belt on her often. She was obviously afraid of him. She describes her mother as psychologically abusive, an unstable woman who had a psychiatric history of her own. More than thirty years after these disturbing childhood experiences, Alice still has nightmares about school and her early home life. Thus, she also shows symptoms of PTSD.

While in therapy, Alice helped to take care of her mom and a disabled sibling. Essentially, these were her only real purposes in life. She never married and had no children. She worked the graveyard shift to maximize pay and benefits, but claimed that monkeys could do the menial factory-type work she was performing. She had no friends and did not trust people in general. She expected to be taken advantage of, just as she had been in the past.

Alice had a long history of alcohol and drug abuse. She said that nothing in life gave her the relief and pleasure she received from alcohol. She knew drugs and alcohol did not mix well with psychiatric medication—so she tried to avoid such medication. She had trouble sleeping, complained of marked feelings of anger, anxiety, and depression, and revealed pessimistic and very sensitive styles of relating to life and people. She could not handle criticism from others and took it as a personal attack and sign that she was incompetent and worthless.

During adolescence and young adulthood, Alice developed a strong indifference to her health and survival. To put it bluntly, she didn't care if she lived or died. Drugs and promiscuity became the major players in her life. Although she never went to jail, she was routinely involved in drunk-and-disorderly episodes. Remarkably, she avoided major setbacks for many years.

Just prior to beginning therapy, Alice became overwhelmed by frustration, hopelessness, and suicidal ideation and was psychiatrically hospitalized. She had been feeling tired and sick much of the time. Medical testing during this period of treatment revealed she was HIV-positive. This condition was actually a relief to her! She initially feared she had cancer. Cancer would probably kill her faster than HIV, so the latter was preferable. She wanted to live long enough to take care of her mom and sibling; they were all that mattered! She did not matter to herself. Alice had not one ounce of concern over the HIV diagnosis. She acknowledged that the condition was probably due to a needle used for drug injections. There was no regret, however, because she saw no value in living, beyond the support of family members.

Alice suffered from subtle suicide for at least a decade. She was intensely ambivalent about living. She had rolled the dice many times in her life and didn't care what the outcome might be. Actually, she would have seen death as a relief (although there was that concern for her mother and brother). Abused as a youngster at home and school, she trusted no one. Her learning and attention disorders added to her inability to relate to others successfully and achieve reasonable life goals. These factors combined to create a hopeless existence with little self-esteem to combat it. The built-in will to survive kept her alive, barely, but overwhelmingly negative thoughts and emotions led to a risky, self-defeating, and destructive lifestyle.

The negative forces eventually won out. She discontinued therapy and disappeared, resurfacing only when her mother died. She was again psychiatrically hospitalized. However, nothing had really changed; she still lived with her brother and was still in a subtly suicidal state and still spiraling downward.

Case Study: Where Do I Fit?

Joe is a young adult who has been in outpatient psychotherapy for some time. He had already seen two other counselors and two psychiatrists and took numerous prescriptions for antidepressants and mood stabilizers without much success. He said the psychiatric medications helped somewhat with his depression, but not his unhappiness. Joe's comment reminds us that depression and unhappiness are relatively independent states, although they overlap. People can be unhappy without being depressed, but clinically depressed people are invariably unhappy. Joe's statement, which separates his depression from his unhappiness, is typical for people suffering from what some call an "existential crisis." Joe, for instance, describes himself as "smart, funny and attractive," yet says, "I can't get myself to feel these ways." At one level of his mind, Joe could describe himself in certain ways, but at another level he could not feel that way.

Joe has a high school education, works full-time, and lives alone. He has several siblings and describes his parents as "average, supportive, and laid back." He has no significant medical problems. He recalls being "normal" until reaching the teen years. During late childhood, he remembers becoming unhappy and introverted. "High school was miserable. I'm glad it's over." Of course, the teen years are when we learn to develop and assert our individuality and identity. We are supposed to become more independent from adults and make increasingly difficult decisions and take responsibility for our decisions. More and more we need to deal with the uncertainties of our social and emotional worlds; we become aware of our vulnerabilities and how alone we often feel.

These existential issues overwhelmed Joe, and he responded in self-defeating and self-destructive manners. He withdrew from others, became dissatisfied with himself, and developed very low self-esteem. Additionally, he felt guilty because he was not "growing" normally. In a classic reaction to his aloneness, low self-esteem, and guilt, he engaged in risky and promiscuous behavior.

During high school, Joe had sex with almost anyone who agreed. The sex of the partner didn't matter much; Joe was simply looking for some type of acceptance and validation. Eventually, alcohol became part of the process. The pattern that developed was one in which he would get drunk on weekend nights and have sex with one or more others before experiencing a blackout. There would be little memory of the events of these evenings. The encounters did not lead to lasting relationships of any kind. He often felt like he allowed others to use his body. There was an empty, lonely feeling that pervaded his life, but he allowed the behavior to continue. He had great difficulty making basic life decisions, even in choosing sexual partners. He merely stated that he was bisexual.

Joe had no clear purpose in life. He admitted to having no dreams or future goals. "I don't see myself living a normal life," he said. During one therapy session, Joe blurted out, "I want to be struck by lightning or have some kind of freak accident."

When asked, "If you didn't wake up tomorrow, would that be okay?" Joe replied, "Well, yeah. I'd be dead, so it wouldn't matter."

"At the end of a tough day, whom can you relate to?" Joe answered, "My cats."

Joe is a prime example of someone in the subtle suicide zone. He wanted to go to college and get out of his dead-end job, but made no efforts along these lines. He wanted to stop drinking and engaging in casual sex on the weekends, but he didn't stop. He wanted some personal goals and plans, but didn't develop any.

As noted, Joe was on several psychiatric medications for his psychological diagnoses, but no medication, of course, will make the changes that he wanted in his life to occur. Combined with psychotherapy, these medicines could potentially help Joe get out of the subtle suicide zone, but the problem is that he shows little regard for himself or his life at this point. More importantly, he is in grave danger of experiencing some form of a major self-destructive act. His promiscuity puts him at high risk for contracting a venereal disease, and his excessive drinking puts him at great risk for being taken advantage of while in a blackout state. His inability to remember what happens on weekend nights makes him an easy target for many types of serious difficulties.

On a more positive note, Joe is willing to admit to psychological problems and seek treatment. There is both time and opportunity for him to reinvent himself. He needs to face the challenges associated with becoming a distinct individual. Joe is an example of how appearances can be deceptive. Similar to people who marry but remain disconnected, he is living alone but not really independently. Joe needs to develop and maintain a focus on plans for the future while not allowing anyone or anything to deter him. Also, he needs to stop allowing himself to engage in demeaning behaviors that lower his self-esteem and put him in serious jeopardy. He needs to muster the courage to make his own decisions for his future and stop escaping from life with risky behaviors that provide minimal growth experiences. If these self-destructive behaviors do not end soon, Joe will probably drift deeper into the subtle suicide zone and find it increasingly difficult to escape.

Case Study: Painful Identity

Ben is in late midlife. He has been psychiatrically hospitalized on many occasions and qualifies for Social Security disability payments for psychiatric reasons. He denies any history of physical, psychological, or sexual abuse. He has one sibling who lives a relatively conventional life, free of any significant psychiatric disturbance. Ben's physical health is relatively good, although he is being treated for high cholesterol.

Ben is thin, short, and frail looking, not the tall, dark, and handsome type. He describes himself as uncoordinated and not at all athletic. No doubt because of his delicate appearance and movements, Ben was teased and bullied a lot as a child. He suffered a great deal of emotional upset from social interactions with his peers, including intense feelings of rejection and embarrassment. He was called many names in school—"geek," "faggot," "nerd." He also recalls feeling "different" from other boys. Eventually, he decided he was homosexual, but he never told anyone about his sexual orientation until well into adulthood. In fact, he was well over forty before his parents found out he was gay.

In typical subtle suicide fashion, Ben's life became one of avoidance and deception. He withdrew from high school during his junior year, even though his grades were okay and his intellectual skills were well above average. He transferred to a technical school and eventually graduated. During his twenties, which he considers his best decade, he drank and partied with friends on a regular basis. He reports drinking a lot and engaging in a good deal of promiscuous behavior during this time. Ultimately, his friends moved away and he became less socially active. His drinking decreased, but he became bored, lonely, and depressed and drifted into gambling and smoking heavily.

During his thirties and forties, Ben slowly fell into the subtle suicide zone where he is today. He has had about a dozen psychiatric hospitalizations, smokes excessively, and most months gambles away his disability check. He is lethargic and depressed most of the time and can't stand the person he has become. He is extremely lonely and has little to look forward to. Ben has little zest for life and acknowledges an intense ambivalence about living. He has not been able to stop his self-destructive and neglectful tendencies, including chain-smoking, gambling, and suicidal thoughts. In addition, he punishes himself regularly with self-demeaning thoughts ("I'm no good"; "All I do is hurt and disappoint others"). He says he would be happy to die if he knew for sure there would be a better place for him upon death. The only things that keep him from overt suicide are his intense fear of death and frequent psychiatric hospitalizations, which give him needed attention, sympathy, and social support.

Ben's prognosis is poor. The part of him that wishes he would die is the same part that makes recovery next to impossible. Unless he becomes determined to stop his self-loathing, eliminate his self-destructive actions, develop more constructive behaviors, and accept that hardship is a necessary part of life, he will not be capable of exiting the subtle suicide zone. Ben still faces the possibility of an endless series of psychiatric hospitalizations that will end only with death, self-destructiveness, or overt suicide.

Case Study: Social Anxiety

Our clinical experiences have taught us that anxiety is as common a problem as depression, but is usually more painful. When we are depressed, as upsetting as this state is, we often don't care about what is happening to us. On the other hand, anxiety is a very agitated, painful experience that is associated with a good deal of caring about what is going on. We get anxious when we feel threatened, which is very uncomfortable. Examples of such discomfort would be when we make a serious mistake, when we are rejected by someone we value, or when we get into an accident. In many ways, anxiety is more painful than depression. Sometimes anxiety and depression occur together; at other times, we seek to avoid anxiety by avoiding responsibility, and the result is depression because our problems just get worse.

We are social animals. We need to be connected to others, and, to a large extent, our life satisfaction is determined by the quality of our social interactions and relationships. This raises an important question: What can happen to people who feel intense anxiety when they are in social situations? The following case is about a woman who developed a serious case of social anxiety and subsequently entered the subtle suicide zone.

Meredith grew up in a secluded, economically and socially depressed small town. She was the oldest of several siblings, and it was her job to help take care of them because Mom worked and Dad was chronically ill. Not surprisingly, Meredith often did not live up to her parents' expectations. Their frequent scolding and criticism did not help her develop much self-esteem. She never really had much self-confidence and grew up believing she was pretty incompetent and unable to meet others' standards.

Meredith's family was poor, and she struggled in school, especially with math and science. She had few opportunities to have fun with friends outside of school and did not have the confidence to build friendships while at school. Thus, she grew up lonely and socially alienated. She admits entering into the subtle suicide zone during the high school years. She always experienced anxiety when she was in the company of others, anxiety that prevented her from having fun. As a result, she felt life was not all that worthwhile, and if she happened to die, so what?

After graduating from high school, Meredith had two failed marriages over the next few years, both to alcoholics. Predictably, she married men who treated her poorly. Because of her childhood, poor treatment is what she expected and, in fact, was the type of treatment she was comfortable with. We have seen this tragic pattern in other cases: people who have psychologically painful experiences in childhood find themselves as adults attracted to partners who recreate that childhood distress. Why? Because the distress is what they are used to dealing with.

Meredith's confidence and self-esteem were so weak that she essentially paid for both divorces and asked for nothing from her ex-husbands. She worked a variety of jobs to support herself, mostly construction, clerical, and factory work. Unfortunately, although she worked extremely hard, she could not get along with coworkers and felt uncomfortable with them. Her social anxiety crippled her in interactions with others, and those around her would usually decide she was some sort of snob who felt above them. In virtually all her jobs, she either quit or was fired, usually the former.

At present, Meredith lives with her grandparents and works in a factory. She still owes money from school loans, and she is very lonely and depressed. She has been psychiatrically hospitalized several times. These hospitalizations seem to give her enough hope to survive, but they don't help her thrive or teach her to confront her problems. Interestingly, Meredith shows a lot of insight into her problems and is able to talk about them openly and frankly: "Everywhere I go I see couples. It seems that there is no one made for me." She adds, "Being alone makes me wonder if I think right." "I pray to die," she says. "Since high school, the world isn't what I thought it would be. I'm tired. I've worked all of my life and have nothing to show for it."

Meredith doesn't want to kill herself, because she is afraid she will go to hell as a sinner. She says, however, that there is no joy in her life, only fear. She admits, "People are my downfall." She doesn't speak with others unless they speak to her first, and at lunchtime, she eats in her car to avoid being around coworkers—actions that just keep her feeling lonely and alienated. She says she doesn't know how to get along with people and thinks that if she tries, she will fail and things will be worse than ever. Meredith has really put herself between a rock and a hard place. She feels so socially inept, and is so afraid of being around others, that she is unwilling to learn how to interact with others and just be herself. Her "I don't care if I live or die" attitude robs her of the motivation to improve her life. A case like this one is very difficult to work with because the social anxiety is so strong.

We don't know how Meredith's case will turn out. She readily admits to believing that people "judge me negatively." This belief isn't paranoia on her part. Rather, the belief is based on being overly sensitive, scared to death of being criticized, and low in self-esteem. Meredith cannot improve unless she gets rid of her paralyzing social anxiety. Only then can she exit the subtle suicide zone. We hope the combination of outpatient therapy and moderate psychiatric medication will help her gain the confidence and skills necessary to have a meaningful social and emotional life.

Case Study: Loss of a Child

We can't think of anything in life more difficult to accept and deal with than the loss of a child. In this case, our client Dorothy's only child committed suicide. Experience has taught us that death of a child by suicide is particularly hard to cope with in comparison with loss due to an accident, illness, or war. In any case, accepting the reality of a child's death is extremely difficult. Many parents say there is a large part of them that simply doesn't even want to attempt to move through the acceptance process, because doing so only reinforces the reality that their child is gone. In these cases, maintaining a sort of denial seems more comforting than doing the hard psychological work of moving toward acceptance, which at best may be more like a form of resignation.

Dorothy experienced a fairly conventional childhood, adolescence, and young adulthood, except that her father was absent during much of this time. Dorothy's lifestyle developed into a caregiver pattern. Growing up, she often had to assume many adult duties to help out her mother, and this pattern persisted as she entered adulthood, married, and began her own family. Dorothy's purpose in life was the care of her family.

Dorothy entered the subtle suicide zone shortly after her adult child committed suicide. The suicide sent her into a major psychological tailspin. She lost interest in almost all activities and began to show signs of severe depression. Several psychiatric hospitalizations followed, and she received psychiatric medication and counseling for the first time in her life. Unfortunately, at first, none of the treatments worked because she no longer cared enough about her own life. In therapy, she showed partial acceptance of her child's suicide, but she also said she didn't see any reason for her to live longer. She wanted to join her child in heaven.

During the several years after her child's death, Dorothy gradually became resigned to the suicide. She felt less guilty and depressed. Like many parents of suicidal children, guilt was a major hurdle to overcome. Dorothy constantly thought of ways she could have prevented the suicide! She had to realize, however, that she was not some psychic who could read the future and control her child's life. Her saving grace was finding comfort in the fact that had she been able to see what was coming, she would have done everything possible to prevent the suicide. As time went on, she blamed herself less, and her depression lifted a bit. But then her father died. She lost the person she considered her best friend and a source of great comfort in her life. Her dad's death reawakened the conflicts and emotions she experienced when her child died; all the months of treatment came unraveled. Plus, now she had an additional reason to die: she could join both her dad and child in heaven.

Dorothy's case is ongoing at this writing. She now feels she has little reason to live. Her purpose in life had always been based on her immediate and extended family, and now crucial parts of both are gone. No amount of medication or psychotherapy could prevent Dorothy from her "I might as well be dead" attitude and descent into the subtle suicide zone. Her situation involves work at developing new purposes, goals, activities, and relationships.

We do not know whether she will exit the subtle suicide zone. She received an incredible amount of support and treatment during her last psychiatric hospitalization. Certainly, we hope she will take advantage of what she gained through these efforts. Because she improved after her child's suicide, her prognosis appears to be fairly good. Her father's death, although a psychological blow, was more expected and natural than her child's death and should, therefore, be easier for her to accept in time. Nevertheless, she still has the same kinds of issues she had before her dad's death. That is, she needs to build her life based upon her own creative purposes and goals. The sooner she gets out of the subtle suicide zone, the better; otherwise, she may continue to spiral downward through self-neglect and self-destructiveness.

Case Study: The Weight of Psychosis

Current psychological theory suggests that psychotic disorders such as schizophrenia are caused by a combination of psychological stress along with psychological and biological predispositions toward this type of illness. Psychologists believe that people differ in their capacity to handle stress without losing touch with reality and withdrawing into a world filled with hallucinations and/or delusions. No psychological disorder is easy to cope with. However, imagine having to deal with one that causes you to see or hear things that are not there. Imagine that no matter how those around you behave, you believe they are plotting against you. Imagine that you are so mentally impaired that you cannot function normally in school, work, or relationships on a day-to-day basis. Because you experience thoughts that others do not, because you see and hear things that others do not, both you and those around you become very uncomfortable. This is the type of case we will discuss next, that of a long-term psychotic, Sally, who began showing psychotic thinking during adolescence.

When Sally entered high school she already had very low self-esteem. Then, she began hearing voices that told her she would suffer the rest of her life because she believed she was no good, and she was going to hell. Her siblings seemed like normal teenagers, but Sally struggled socially and had no real friends in high school. Although she graduated and subsequently married, she began to use drugs and alcohol excessively, mostly to try to get away from the troubling voices. After having a child, Sally stopped her drug and alcohol abuse and sought medical treatment. She took many prescription psychiatric medications to help subdue the voices, but none of them helped for any length of time. The voices always returned, and she needed to be psychiatrically hospitalized many times.

Sally admitted that her only reason for living during her twenties and thirties was her child. Most other aspects of her life were a mess. She got divorced, was unable to hold down a steady job, and lived at the poverty level. She received some support from her parents, but she had no significant friendships and no real goals or purposes in life. On top of all these stresses, the voices pounded her constantly, causing significant additional distress. At times, the voices were relentless, and Sally was desperate to stop them and the psychological pain they brought her.

Presently in therapy, Sally travels through life with paralyzing fears and intense feelings of worthlessness. Her parents, members of her therapy group, and hospital therapeutic staff give her as much support as they can, but she continues to battle subtle suicide. She does not really want to die, but then again she has no strong motive to live, either. In her mind, her best hope is the advent of some new medication that will get rid of the voices.

A major problem in treating Sally is that the development of meaningful goals and purposes in life seems absurd to her at the present time. She sees all such goals as unattainable; the voices are too strong. The intensity of her battle is represented nicely in the movie *A Beautiful Mind*, based on the real-life struggles of the brilliant economist John Nash. As for Sally, our hope is that she may be able to develop some "minor," day-to-day goals that might give her hope that she can learn to cope with her psychotic symptoms. These small steps just might provide her with sufficient motivation and incentive to want to live more than to give up and die.

Case Study: The Gambler

This case provides a good example of how a victim spirals downward once entering and remaining in the subtle suicide zone. The case also shows how a symptomatic behavior—in this case, gambling—is not the true core conflict that must be addressed.

Zach's father abandoned the family when Zach was just a child, and he grew up with an alcoholic mother who had a gambling problem. Throughout childhood and into his teen years and young adulthood, Zach was a bright and outgoing individual who succeeded academically and socially. He developed a close friendship with Kyle, one of his peers, and was pretty much "adopted" by Kyle's family. He spent a lot of time with this family. Kyle and Kyle's dad became like a brother and father to Zach.

After graduating from college, Zach and Kyle worked at Kyle's family business. They worked hard and were successful. They both showed interest in making the business their life's work, and their careers seemed set. However, there were underlying and potentially destructive psychological issues within Zach. Although he had married by now and had a wonderful wife and children, Zach had serious unresolved issues from his childhood and adolescence. The sense of aloneness as a result of his father leaving, and the lack of warmth and nurturance from his mother, left him with unresolved emotional issues.

Zach spent most of his life avoiding these issues and the insecurities they caused him. He probably didn't appreciate or understand how powerful these issues were or the fact that they prevented him from ever truly sharing himself fully with anyone and trusting others. Zach seemed to be living the American dream: a nice house, bright and healthy kids, a good job, and a loving wife. The truth is, however, that Zach felt empty and alone; his success and loving family were not enough for him. In fact, his deep unresolved conflicts and insecurities insured he would *never* feel he had enough. The psychological hole he developed over time could not be filled with adult success because he was too busy running from his childhood insecurities.

For many years at Kyle's family business, Zach worked very hard and put his heart into the business. However, he slowly began to get involved in his own get-rich-quick schemes and developed a serious gambling problem. He developed wild fantasies of getting filthy rich and powerful and being treated by others as a brilliant and masterful businessman. Realistically, of course, his chances of reaching these goals were very low, but Zach was not one to be bothered with harsh realities. He even admitted to friends, "No amount of money could ever be enough for me."

His risky schemes and gambling got worse with time, and he had to borrow large sums of money, most of which he never paid back. Zach slowly began to alienate his family, Kyle, coworkers, and friends. Over more than a decade, he took advantage of many people due to his gambling. Problems and pressures grew. On more than one occasion, Zach quit his job, only to return days later asking to be reinstated. The time came, however, when he was finally told that he would not be accepted back at work. Gambling became more difficult, too. Bookies no longer advanced him credit and told him he needed to pay up. Family and friends stopped lending him money. Soon, Zach faced bankruptcy, loss of his home, public shame, and embarrassment. During this time, he consulted a priest and psychologist, but he never really fully opened up to either about the real nature of his psychological problems. He was never sufficiently motivated to confront his fears.

It is ironic that Zach, who was so successful as a student, family man, and worker, still felt unworthy of love and distrustful of others. If only he could have faced up to his fundamental fear of rejection and abandonment, he could have related to both himself and others in more positive ways. By the time he sought some counseling, however, he had been in the subtle suicide zone for too long. He had spiraled down so far he could not motivate himself to work consistently enough to change. He could see no way out of emotional and financial ruin. He was alone with his problems, and his life would end the same way.

One day Zach's wife came home and found him dead by his own hand. There was no note; there were no good-byes. From Zach's perspective, there was no more pain for him. He no longer needed to avoid unpleasant thoughts and feelings. Memories of his father's abandonment and painful comparisons of his life to Kyle's did not have to be endured any longer. Zach quit on his wife and kids the way his dad had quit on him. Ultimately, he became caught in a vicious cycle of self-destruction that led to his death. He was filled with too much anxiety, depression, guilt, anger, shame, low self-esteem, hopelessness, narcissism, and self-defeating actions to overcome the conflicts and fears that had begun decades earlier.

After Zach's death, the psychologist interviewed Kyle, explained subtle suicide to him, and asked him if he had seen signs of this pattern in Zach. Kyle said that during the past several years that Zach had worked with him, Zach had definitely descended into a self-destructive pattern that no one seemed to understand. No matter how Kyle or his family tried to support Zach and understand what was going on, Zach kept up his self-defeating and self-destructive behavior patterns. His decisions made little sense, unless we conclude that Zach, feeling alone and unwanted, was hell-bent on self-destruction and had been for many years.

Case Study: Devastating Loss and Loneliness

Catastrophic sickness is not the only trauma that can push someone into the subtle suicide zone. Equally devastating can be the sudden loss of someone who plays a vital role in one's life. Martha's case illustrates this latter example quite well and also shows how counseling can be used to help a person cope with subtle suicide tendencies.

Martha, in her late fifties, had always lived quietly with her homosexuality. She was not one to announce or otherwise display her sexual preference. For years, she had a stable and intimate relationship with her partner. However, the partner had died suddenly a few years earlier, and Martha was emotionally devastated. The fact that she lived and worked in a small town, far from larger metropolitan areas where there would be more support from a gay/lesbian population, just added to her adjustment difficulties. Also, her age made it very difficult for her to meet available gays in her own small community. Over time, she became more and more depressed over her personal loss, as well as extremely lonely and longing for affection. She gradually drifted into a subtle suicide condition over the next several years. She didn't care about living and became vulnerable to risky, careless behavior patterns. For instance, a neighbor woman became interested in her. Almost sixty years of age and desperate for a love connection, Martha developed an intimate relationship despite her better judgment (the neighbor was married).

A few years later, while in therapy, Martha admitted that her subtle suicide condition at this time allowed her to behave in very uncharacteristic ways. Martha entered counseling because her married partner rejected her after more than three years of involvement. Although angry and upset over the way the relationship ended, she was no longer subtly suicidal. Martha's relationship, as inappropriate as it was, brought her out of the subtle suicide condition. What is also interesting is the fact that when the relationship ended, she did not drift back into the subtle suicide zone. One reason is the fact that she sought counseling when the relationship ended, and she was able to face many of her fears.

Martha also realizes she is at risk for drifting back into subtle suicide if she is not careful. Her awareness of the subtle suicide process, as well as the fact that she is presently in counseling, decreases the likelihood that she will fall back into subtle suicide in the future. In her case, therefore, the purpose of counseling is primarily prevention, not treatment. Martha needs to be guided into constructive ways of coping with her loneliness and depression. At the same time, she needs to avoid self-defeating actions that could make her even more depressed and produce other negative emotional states such as anxiety, frustration, and anger. Martha is learning that she needs to accept her sadness and loneliness and get better control over both her thinking and her actions. She is focusing on these two factors she can control. For instance, she can stop obsessing (something she can control) over the behavior of others (something she can't control). That focus is helping her to stop feeling sorry for herself and encourages her to reach out and meet new people who can give her more positive life experiences.

Case Study: Devastating Loss and Modeling

Martha's main problem after her loss was loneliness. In Arnold's case, however, we see different reactions at work. The result, however—falling into the subtle suicide zone—is the same.

Arnold's sister accidentally died when they were both teenagers. Arnold tried to save her but failed. Arnold, in fact, almost died during his rescue efforts. Over the years, the family never really talked about what happened, their intense sense of loss and sadness, or how they felt about the failed rescue attempt. These actions represent a type of denial and withdrawal from the reality of the situation, of course, and this lack of communication put great strain on the family. The mother became an alcoholic and was in and out of psychiatric hospitals and drug and alcohol treatment programs for many years. She was never able to accept the loss of her child and move on with her life in a constructive manner. Arnold's father buried himself in his work and focused on being the main provider for the family. Arnold became a surrogate parent to his two younger siblings and also developed problems with alcohol.

Initially, Arnold slowly began to relate to the loss by deciding he was partially responsible for his sister's death. As a result, he became filled with shame and guilt. Arnold came to believe that he should have died, not his sister. Therefore, he decided he did not deserve to live or be happy. Nothing he could do would bring his sister back, of course, and Arnold had no one around to help him process his thoughts and emotions in a more appropriate way. Because the family didn't discuss these important issues and he was not in counseling, Arnold had to live with his simplistic and self-critical thought patterns. These feelings are really not that unusual, and we saw similar reactions of shame and guilt in a previous case study. Arnold's case, however, also shows us how modeling, or following the reactions of others, can also be involved in the subtle suicide process.

Many cases of subtle suicide involve the victim modeling the behavior of someone else, and we see this example with Arnold being influenced by his mother's reactions to the accidental death. Arnold and his mother shared the common experience of failing to save a family member. Both experienced guilt and both took care of the youngest children in the home. Both also eventually became alcoholics.

Arnold identified strongly with his mother and followed many of her paths. He felt intense guilt and shame and tried to suppress these emotions. Like his mom, he avoided talking about his feelings, and he turned to alcohol to cope with his pain. Both eventually turned to therapy, and the mother eventually gave up her dependence on alcohol and moved on more constructively with her life.

Arnold, however, struggled with his alcoholism and developed some chronic medical problems due to alcohol abuse. There were also some psychological diagnoses that took his treatment off track. He was diagnosed with many different psychological disorders, including bipolar disorder and alcohol dependence. In our opinion, though, these diagnostic and treatment approaches missed the point by a wide margin. Arnold suffered with PTSD, which instilled in him feelings of helplessness about events in his life. These feelings led him to a "What does it matter?" attitude about his life and whether he lives or dies. Early treatment of these reactions, rather than concentrating on the alcohol problems and a bipolar diagnosis (plus psychiatric medications), might have made a difference for Arnold and kept him out of the subtle suicide zone.

His therapist helped Arnold focus on how his subtle suicide condition developed and what he needs to do to recover. Arnold eventually decided that it was time to face his psychological problems head-on. The first step he took was to slowly wean himself from the many numbing psychiatric medications he had been put on for his various psychiatric diagnoses. The medications were simply doing pretty much the same thing that alcohol did—that is, help him avoid confronting his guilt and shame.

Arnold began to understand that he needed to do more for himself if he expected to get better. Put another way, he had to develop his own purposes and goals in order to live a more valued life. He also had to accept the fact that he was not responsible for his sister's death and that he is just as deserving to be happy as anyone else. He needed to see that he had been putting the brakes on his growth and happiness for some time, and that only he could stop his self-destructive actions.

Arnold is currently married, unemployed, and in therapy. He spends most of his time at home providing for his children. Arnold's story is not over, and we don't know how the final chapter will read. However, we believe he finally has a fighting chance, because his complicated history and emotional issues are in focus. He understands that if he does not commit himself to living life more fully, subtle suicide will likely take him down.

PERSONALITY DYSFUNCTIONS

Case Study: Borderline Personality

Borderline personalities do not have an integrated and unified sense of self. In many respects, they retain childlike qualities in adulthood. They are impulsive, show poor mood regulation, express excessive fear of abandonment, react immaturely to stress, and have difficulty maintaining smooth and intimate relationships. Generally they see things in black-and-white terms, so they have trouble compromising and changing their actions. Their emotions and behaviors tend to be extreme and self-destructive in the long run.

The causes of borderline personality disorder are complex, but many theorists focus on dysfunctional parent–child relations. The family background of borderline clients usually involves parents who are inconsistent in their behavior, do not provide clear expectations for the child, and fail to provide appropriate love and support. For example, a mother might alternate from being overly protective and emotionally suffocating to being excessively cold, critical, and demanding. The father, meanwhile, might remain aloof and distant, almost emotionally neutral. This type of parenting can foster a child who has difficulty with self-acceptance, strong fears of abandonment, and low-esteem. Many borderline individuals also show subtle suicide characteristics, involving self-destructive acts such as an eating disorder, self-mutilation, gambling, suicidal acts, and drug or alcohol abuse.

Let's consider Emily, who sought treatment after psychiatric hospitalization. She was married and had children and described her marriage and family life in positive terms. She worked part-time and had plans to go back to school to complete career plans. For a time, she was involved with and dependent on a small group of people at a new church, a fundamentalist religious sect. The members treated her much like her mother had when Emily was a child. Her husband felt her association with this group was very risky for her emotionally and eventually convinced her to leave the group with the support of her counselor.

Emily had struggled with obesity most of her life, and she readily admitted to a history of bulimia. Although her eating disorder was now a thing of the past, cutting and self-mutilating behaviors were not. She minimized the extent of her cutting, but reluctantly admitted she still sliced her arms and stomach areas. Sometimes the cutting was deep enough to require medical attention. In addition, she had a history of overdosing on various medications, mostly nonpsychiatric ones.

Emily's childhood had been filled with fear. She remembered hiding alone in her room as a child for long periods of time. Apparently, she desperately wanted to avoid the conflict and disapproval so prevalent in her home life. She remembers her mother as very critical and disapproving. Her dad was not around much because of work. When he was, he allowed her mom to be the unquestioned master of the house. Mom was often a screamer, and Emily hid to avoid her screaming.

Emily was the middle child and always felt her siblings were favored, with Mom preferring one and Dad the other. This perception, right or wrong, didn't help her self-esteem or feelings of being unloved and rejected. Shame also played a role. Emily was the only fat one in the family! The more she worried about her weight, the more she ate. She had become an emotional eater. Stress, not hunger, fueled her desire for food. Eating became the most consistent and convenient way to soothe herself, but it was enormously self-defeating and self-damaging.

Another significant factor related to shame revolved around sexual abuse by a relative when Emily was in early childhood. She vaguely remembers these episodes but doesn't know how many there were. The full realization of the abuse came to her when she was thirteen. Her sister told her about a dream involving a relative in her bed. Realizing the infinitesimally low odds that her sister would have the same type of "dream," they eventually confronted their parents. The parents acknowledged such an event had in fact occurred and that the relative had been banned from the household.

Once Emily was in therapy as an adult, she began to understand the true impact of what happened. She was able to see that various childhood events affected her ability to be close to her dad and other men and made her feel ashamed and unworthy. For years during childhood, she questioned why she had such strange memories and feelings. At thirteen, she finally learned why, but the damage was done.

As years passed, Emily's life path stayed on course. Although she seemed "normal," subtle suicide tendencies lay dormant. She alternated between loving and hating life and herself. Getting married and having children helped settle her down somewhat, but she became codependent on her husband, who was often unavailable emotionally. It wasn't easy for him to ride her emotional roller coaster.

Marriage and motherhood also gave Emily more reasons to fear rejection and expect abandonment. Moreover, living close to her siblings and parents helped strengthen her disapproval, distrust, and abandonment issues. Whenever she sought advice or support from family, she was treated like she was when she was a child. Thus, a vicious cycle emerged: she continued to display childlike behaviors while receiving scolding responses from family members, especially her mom, which led her to more childlike behaviors.

During therapy, Emily often played the parent/child game, trying to elicit verbal reprimands from the therapist as if the therapist was the parent scolding her, the child. She literally tried to entice the therapist into responding like a disapproving parent. It wasn't easy, but the therapist resisted and tried to guide her into seeing how her behavior was reproducing the patterns of her childhood, including avoiding responsibility and showing self-destructive actions. She had little self-respect, did not feel in control of her life, and had strong subtle suicide tendencies.

Emily had a lot of stress and pain to avoid. She was obese, depressed, and excessively dependent on others for approval and attention. Still, what was the point of sitting on the subtle suicide fence? She was neither moving forward with her life in positive ways nor ending it. She was wasting a lot of time and psychological energy.

Emily and her therapist discussed the notion of subtle suicide. She did not fight the possibility that the profile fit her, but she was very slow to change her behaviors in positive ways. She still had much to fear. The little girl in her wanted to retreat to her room, but now there was no such place for her to hide. She vacillated greatly and even needed brief psychiatric hospitalization while in therapy. She continued to work, however, and attend college for career advancement. These positive activities gave her therapist something to work with in showing Emily how she could exercise more control in her life.

Another area of control was Emily's dysfunctional marriage, which reinforced the fears of rejection and abandonment she had experienced as a child. Once she confronted these issues, she decided to leave her husband. The marriage never really met her basic wants and needs for growth and self-acceptance. Her decision to leave him was huge because she was confronting her childhood fears for the first time, and that decision helped move her out of the subtle suicide zone.

Emily's family had a difficult time supporting her decision to leave her husband. They were afraid she needed him and couldn't make it on her own, and her past behaviors were consistent with these fears. It wasn't easy, but Emily learned to live and parent alone. She changed jobs several times and had to learn how to face life without the safety net her husband had provided. Although she knew she could rely on her parents if absolutely necessary, she wanted to succeed on her own.

As Emily made progress in becoming more independent, her self-esteem increased and her self-destructive behaviors decreased. She even lost considerable weight through a program that required significant eating and lifestyle changes. It took years of therapy, but Emily was finally able to leave the subtle suicide zone. Sometimes her desires to cut herself and overeat returned, even when she had no significant distress. She came to realize that her self-destructive behavior patterns had become habitual. Furthermore, she realized that subtle suicide behaviors set in motion a vicious cycle that sent her tumbling downward. Disrespecting her body caused shame, humiliation, and lowered self-esteem that made it more likely she would continue such self-damaging and self-sabotaging behaviors. Only she could break the cycle by discontinuing the self-mutilating acts. This realization helped her do so. Emily also helped herself by realizing that she sought sympathy and attention by engaging in self-injurious acts. She didn't believe others would show true interest in her or give attention unless she created a reason for them to do so.

Emily finally understood she needed to stop her life-versus-death conflict. She was able to make the life force dominant, but only with a lot of help and motivated effort on her part. Disengaging somewhat from her parents and leaving her husband proved essential for her growth. She needed to develop an independent and positive identity, which was impossible until she made these separations. Yes, she will struggle with her issues for the rest of her life, but she is no longer at the mercy of these problems because she finally has decided to control them.

Case Study: The Antisocial Personality

Not all subtle suicide victims seek treatment for their psychological problems. Antisocial personalities (sometimes referred to as *sociopaths*) are one type of individual who rarely enters treatment voluntarily. Many are incarcerated in prisons and, generally, enter a form of treatment only when required by some type of legitimate authority.

Generally speaking, antisocial personalities are impulsive and rebellious and have a low frustration tolerance. They manipulate others without feeling any guilt about it. They see others as pawns to be used and have difficulty establishing and maintaining intimate relationships. They take a lot of risks, even illegal ones, but don't worry much about the consequences of their actions. They resent authority figures and show a lot of hostility toward people in charge.

The case that follows concerns Brian, a middle-aged man with strong antisocial tendencies. He has been married twice and has numerous children from different women, none of whom he is close with. He presently lives alone.

Brian grew up in a home with a sister and his natural parents. His father was both physically and verbally abusive toward everyone in the family, and the mother sometimes displaced her anger toward her husband on the children. In a nutshell, Brian's family life was full of conflict and hostility; expressions of affection were rare in this cold atmosphere.

As a teenager, Brian desperately wanted to leave home, and in his late teens he joined the military. The military afforded him money, as well as the structure and organization he needed. Although he didn't like having to follow so many rules, his behavior was better than at home because in the military he had little choice but to be obedient. He was smart, skilled, and performed well in the military, moving up the ranks fairly quickly. However, along the way he began to drink and smoke heavily. Sexually, he was very promiscuous. When driving, he was fast and reckless and had many accidents, one of which almost killed him. Eventually he married and started a family, but his reckless behavior patterns continued, including having a lot of extramarital affairs.

As a young man and soldier, Brian had no idea how to be a husband and father. Furthermore, he had little respect for the law, his wife, people in general, or even himself. He was filled with so much anger and bitterness that he couldn't even love his own children. People were objects to be used at his pleasure, like chess pieces. He constantly made empty promises, displayed phony expressions of regret, and used others to his advantage. His disdain for others was exceeded only by his dislike for himself.

Brian never came to grips with his rough childhood or his negative feelings toward his family. His life became one of avoiding and escaping the discomfort of his early life. Over the years, his drinking increased, and he had sex with an incredible number of women. Even though HIV and other sexually transmitted diseases were well known, he ignored the risks. After getting divorced from his first wife, he met a woman who was getting out of her first marriage. She was "on the rebound," and he manipulated and charmed her. Eventually, filled with doubts and misgivings, she agreed to marry him.

They had a child, but after putting his best foot forward for some time, Brian resorted to his old ways. Soon he was seeing other women, abusing his wife psychologically and physically, drinking huge amounts of alcohol, chain-smoking, and getting into intense conflicts and fights with his father, strangers in bars, and even his so-called friends.

Eventually, wife number two gave Brian his walking papers and left the country. She took their child with her (with his permission) and began a new life with another man. The split sent Brian into an even deeper fall into subtle suicide. He was forced to resign from his military position as a major because he had become derelict in duty. His drinking and smoking accelerated, and others could see he was aging quickly. Even though his ex-wife moved on with her life, Brian continued calling her to see if she would come back to him. He couldn't understand how and why he let the best thing in his life go. He was becoming totally isolated. Around this time, his father died, and he found himself with no real friends or positive emotional relationships with his family or children.

Brian's subtle suicide behaviors have brought him to a position where he has little to live or hope for. There is always the possibility he could still change his life and develop some integrity and happiness. Realistically, however, this change is all but impossible. He not only has extremely negative attitudes about himself and others, but his ways of behaving are also both strong and negative. He failed to deal with his resentment toward his parents, a failure that locked him into a pattern of using others for his personal gain. Because he has few reasons to live and has strong antisocial personality tendencies in his relations with others, he is extremely unlikely to change. Brian is not the type of person who profits from therapy; he has no remorse or regret over how he has abused himself and others.

Presently, Brian has only a lifetime of regrets to look forward to. He lives for the pleasure of the moment, one day at a time, continuing to be destructive to himself and others while attempting to avoid thinking about his past. It is just a matter of time until he goes down. The only question is how and when. He is his own worst enemy. His case is a good example of how people who don't respect others cannot respect themselves. Lack of self-respect allows such people to take chances with their own health and well-being while hurting others in the process. Like Brian, someday they will die from a cigarette- or alcohol-related malady, STD, jealous lover, or by some other unnecessary means.

Case Study: The Narcissist

Anyone who works in the mental health field for very long knows narcissistic personalities rarely kill themselves. They simply consider themselves too "special" to do such a thing. Ironically, they cannot stand criticism from others, but they readily damage themselves through neglect, denial, possessiveness, and other self-defeating ways of coping. Over a long period of time, their distorted thoughts and inappropriate behavioral patterns can lead to significant deterioration in many areas of essential functioning. Such downfalls can help these types enter the subtle suicide zone.

Narcissists comprise about 1 percent of the adult population and show the following personality characteristics: sense of entitlement, lack of empathy, extreme difficulty handling criticism, an exaggerated sense of self-importance, possessiveness, strong needs for attention and admiration, and a tendency to exploit others. Narcissists tend to devalue others in order to help maintain their own inflated sense of self.

Martin is in his mid-forties. He was married once, for less than a year, and had one child. His reasons for entering treatment revolved around his relationship with his college-age son, Bill. They were close but often fought and argued. It was clear that Bill was growing weary of Martin's narcissism. Psychological assessment showed that Martin and Bill had similar personalities. Martin, however, was more depressed and narcissistic. Both were considerably overweight, although Martin was morbidly obese, almost three hundred pounds overweight. They had decided to go for gastric bypass surgery together, but Martin backed out at the last minute.

Martin was the youngest of several siblings. He was spoiled and treated like a "mascot." Though he developed into an intelligent and educated man, his narcissistic qualities eventually alienated him from others. His possessiveness, for instance, created a great deal of ambivalence for Bill. Although he loved his dad, Bill also wanted to develop his independence and individuality. He wanted to go away to college, but resisted because it would require moving away from home. Martin tried to manipulate Bill into going to school near home. Martin had become so obese that he was confined to a wheelchair most of the time, making him quite dependent on Bill. He made Bill feel guilty about leaving by playing the "sick" role in attempts to get attention and sympathy. In narcissistic fashion, he cleverly conveyed the message to Bill that, as a needy father, his needs should be put above Bill's. Bill would be irresponsible if he deserted him by going away to college.

Martin had a history of psychiatric hospitalizations, and he had been diagnosed with bipolar disorder several years earlier. At the time, he was having difficulty sleeping and suffered from intense mood fluctuations. He was given a number of psychotropic medications, including a mood stabilizer, and was referred for appropriate outpatient treatment. He continued to gain weight, however, and became less and less able to get around. Also, he developed many medical problems and always seemed to have a lot of aches and pains. Independent living became harder and harder. He could not work, and he slowly became quite dependent on Bill (and constantly reminded Bill of that fact!).

Both Martin and Bill got involved in therapy. Unfortunately, not much was resolved for Martin. Bill, on the other hand, received some help with future decisions. For Bill, counseling occurred before his lifestyle became too habitual, so it was easier for him to make positive changes. He was able to overcome his guilt over moving out of the house to complete a college education. Bill began to progress and took steps to assume greater control over his decisions. For Martin, however, the subtly suicidal one, life was going in the opposite direction—downward! Soon, he needed another psychiatric hospitalization.

During the next several years, Martin saw other health professionals, and they changed his diagnosis to major depression and personality disorder "not otherwise specified." Presumably, this change in diagnosis occurred because he failed to respond favorably to the dozen or more prescription psychiatric medications, along with the many hours of individual and group therapy. Martin also complained of frequent suicidal thoughts and overdosed several times on various medications. He had also been charged with forging checks and stealing money. The downward spiral accelerated when he had to live alone after Bill went off to college, a few hours away. Ultimately, Martin had to resign himself to living in a personal care home. He simply could not exit the subtle suicide zone he had entered years before. He also continued to gorge himself with food in self-destructive fashion.

Martin's case gives us some important lessons. First of all, narcissists like him can be very self-defeating and self-destructive because they tend to see themselves as special; they do not see rules and guidelines set by the realities of life as applying to them. In Martin's case, he simply acted as though he was entitled to do whatever he wanted, all the while expecting he would avoid suffering any negative consequences for his self-defeating behaviors. This approach to life led to a quick divorce and extreme possessiveness and exploitation in relation to his only child, Bill, who was made to feel responsible for chores that should have been taken care of by Martin. For example, Bill cooked their meals, cleaned the house, and took Martin to his medical appointments. Obviously, this arrangement did not produce a positive father–son relationship. More importantly, Martin's "I'm special" attitude with respect to eating gave him many significant health problems. His attitude was that, whereas *other* people needed to watch their weight, he could eat as much as he wanted, whenever he wanted! This attitude led to a much lower quality of life and a deflated sense of self-esteem.

Usually, narcissists can avoid severe depression with their manipulations of other people and their ability to use denial and avoidance. Martin, however, could not succeed in avoiding serious problems because of his self-destructive eating. He hated his physical appearance and lack of mobility. He had been a physically attractive man and now had trapped himself in an ugly, huge body. On a daily basis, he had a lot of physical discomfort and suffered frustration over not being able to do many day-to-day activities. With Bill's departure to college, he was also alone and pretty much without hope.

A second lesson in this case is that personality disorders are very hard to treat, especially if they are severe and not addressed effectively early in life. By the time of our contact with Martin, he was already physically disabled, financially strapped, and severely narcissistic. His problems had been going on for many years. When problems and personality patterns have persisted for a long time, even long-term intense therapy may not yield positive results. Martin's narcissistic spiral had taken him too deep into the subtle suicide zone. He didn't have the motivation to kill himself, but he showed a capacity to slowly end his life through self-neglect and self-abuse. Who knows how many years he has taken off his life because of obesity, medication abuse, and associated self-defeating behaviors? What is certain is that he lowered the quality of his life immeasurably because of his narcissistic behavior.

MEDICAL COMPLICATIONS

Case Study: Struggling to Die and Overwhelmed by Stress

Samantha was a teenager when her mother finally drank and smoked herself to death before reaching forty. Samantha then had to become a surrogate mother for her two younger siblings. She finished high school, married, and had three children of her own. Unfortunately, her husband was often too ill to work, and Samantha had little choice but to do factory work and still be the primary caretaker at home, plus taking care of her father who eventually moved in.

Samantha was fifty when her father and husband died less than two months apart. Adding to her grief were her incurable lung conditions, a fungal infection in one lung and a bacterial infection in the other. Her doctor told her to stop smoking if she wanted to live, but she made only half-hearted attempts to stop, and never succeeded.

For the next three years, Samantha lived on public assistance and Social Security benefits because she was disabled and could not work. Furthermore, her adult children had social, emotional, and legal difficulties, mainly associated with relationship problems. One offspring returned to live with her and caused additional financial and other stressors. Samantha became more and more socially withdrawn, even from family members. Just prior to entering the hospital for the last time, she put an inscription on her husband's gravesite which read something like: "If I could, I would climb up all the steps to heaven just to get you back again." In self-destructive fashion, she failed to apply for a supplement to Medicare, thus preventing her from getting medicine for treatment of her lung-related symptoms. She complained of being tired and depressed most of the time and, not surprisingly, continued to smoke feverishly.

Upon entering the hospital, Samantha kissed her grandchildren goodbye and told her sons at her bedside that she was going to die. She refused food and signed a "do not resuscitate" order. When put on a respirator, she became angry, saying, "I want to go!"

In retrospect, it is clear that Samantha had grown weary of poor health, financial problems, and family-related stress. Her purpose for living was also diminished by her father's and husband's deaths, along with her children reaching adulthood. She knew she was killing herself with cigarettes and poor medication management, but she refused to change. She was more motivated to die than to live. She didn't want help to change; she simply wanted to be released from life. It is doubtful that therapy would have made much of a difference for Samantha. Although not overtly suicidal, Samantha nevertheless suffered a subtle suicide death.

Case Study: Chronic Illness

Will learned early in life that the world can be a tough place. His mother and father fought frequently, and eventually Dad walked out for good. While growing up, Will had minimal contact with his father, and the dominant male figure in his life became his stepfather, Justin. Justin had contact with many people through his business, and his customers generally liked him. At home, however, Justin could be described as intimidating, crude, hostile, and a drunk. It was not uncommon for him to physically and psychologically abuse Will. The long and short of it was that Will reports being physically abused by his stepfather, emotionally deprived by his biological father, and figuratively abandoned by his mother.

Understandably, Will struggled during his early and middle childhood years. He had low self-esteem, many exaggerated fears, and a distrust of others, and he was easily intimidated. However, when he reached puberty, things changed in many ways. Will grew rapidly into a manlike body, learned self-defense, and exercised for hours at a time. His self-esteem and social standing with peers grew during his late teens and young adult years. He learned to funnel his anger and fear into constructive pursuits. Ultimately, he acquired a good job, participated in professional athletics, and entered marathons to keep in shape. He was no longer afraid of his father or stepfather; in fact, he was afraid of no man.

Will's physique and athletic prowess made him the envy of many men and the target of a lot of women. He kept on track with a healthy lifestyle while avoiding temptations and self-destructive excesses. Eventually, he met the all-American gal, got married, and had children. He was living the dream, but then things began to unravel. Around the time of his first child's birth, Will became very ill and almost died. He spent almost two months in the hospital with a chronic disease, much of that time in intensive care. He was shocked that almost no one, including family members, visited him while he lay in a hospital bed with tubes coming in and out of various parts of his body. It was as if he was no longer of any use to others because he had a major physical flaw.

Although he survived the ordeal, follow-up treatments required him to be on massive amounts of anti-inflammatory medication. These medications caused considerable weight gain even though he reduced his calorie intake significantly. Almost overnight he went from a well-sculpted marathoner to an obese ex-athlete. To add insult to injury, his marriage suffered because he wasn't the man he used to be. This marital strain was hard for him to accept, because he didn't feel he deserved a poor marriage.

Will eventually was able to return to work, but new stresses developed there. Because he refused to give in to coworkers and sign documents that would allow state property to be stolen from his workplace, he became the object of rejection, criticism, intimidation, and threats. When the company and workers came under investigation, Will testified against his coworkers in court and was vindicated. However, retaliation and harassment at work quickly followed. One of the tires fell off his car shortly after he left work one day; on another occasion, he found all his tires flattened in the parking lot when he was ready to go home. Will also had a lot of financial problems resulting from the retaliations in the workplace.

After about ten years, the pressure of all of these stressors finally got to him. He came to feel that the only reasons to live were his children. Most friends, family, and coworkers who had supported and socialized with him before he became ill were now nowhere to be found, and he felt abandoned. He became demoralized and worn down by the tremendous stress, which was difficult to handle because of minimal support systems and his medical condition. Ironically, he had survived an emotionally abusive childhood only to find it recreated in the workplace.

The combined stressors finally drove Will to therapy. It didn't take long to see that he was in the subtle suicide zone and had been for some time. He admitted to abusing alcohol on a regular basis. Frequently, he took various prescription medications while under the influence of alcohol, thinking it would be okay if he didn't wake up. He had come to believe that the wife and kids would be fine financially without him, and he would be relieved of his pain and suffering.

Although individual therapy did not remove him from the subtle suicide zone, it did clarify his conflicts and provided a safe and supportive environment from which to explore his feelings, attitudes, and values. Additionally, therapy helped drain off some of the huge amounts of frustration and anger that had built up over many years. He told the therapist things he had never said to anyone before, including describing traumatic experiences from his childhood. He and his therapist developed trust through authentic encounters. Will was not the type of man who would normally enter into therapy voluntarily. However, these were far from normal circumstances, and he knew he needed help to get through them, just as he needed doctors to help get him through intensive care with his chronic illness. There was a part of him that still wanted to live and see his kids grow up, despite all the stress, pain, and medical problems he endured.

One day, everything came to a head. He had drunk too much the night before and felt horrible in the morning. The combination of stress, exhaustion, lack of sleep, medical conditions, and being hung over made him feel like he was dying both physically and psychologically. He went to his therapist's office for help, but it was a weekend and the therapist was out of town. A colleague was available, however, and he listened to Will.

Sizing up the situation quickly and accurately, the doctor recommended that Will voluntarily enter a psychiatric facility that day. Shortly thereafter, they spoke to his psychologist on his phone and all agreed hospitalization was appropriate. This event became a major turning point for Will.

Although he stayed in the psychiatric facility for only a few days, Will came out a changed man. Psychiatric hospitalization was a huge wake-up call. He saw patients there who were much less fortunate and capable, and he began to appreciate his freedom. He hated being locked up and at the mercy of doctors who thought they understood him. At the same time, he felt a bond with some of the patients, which made him feel less alone with his problems.

Will quickly became preoccupied with the desire to get out of the hospital so he could get on with his life. He became less depressed about the state of his marriage; if things didn't improve, he could accept that. The important thing was the welfare of his kids. He faced the subtle suicide process directly and decided he wanted to live more than he wanted to die. He became more determined to accept mistreatment in the work environment without taking his anger out on himself. He decided to stop drinking alcohol and return to a more healthy lifestyle. Because he continued to have pressures and struggles both at home and at work, he continued with his therapy for support. However, he was no longer ambivalent about living; he was no longer in the subtle suicide zone.

Will's case illustrates a number of issues with respect to treatment of subtle suicide victims. First of all, Will's subtle suicide slowly but steadily developed from many factors, including physical and emotional abuse during childhood, severe medical problems, and both occupational and marital stresses. Second, individual therapy was helpful in developing trust in the therapist and finding a valuable ally. Third, therapy helped Will clarify and understand many of the emotional conflicts he had, conflicts that went all the way back to his early family life. Therapy gave Will a chance to express his long-suppressed emotions and get some release from the psychological pressure he had been living with for many years. Ultimately, however, it was psychiatric hospitalization that was the catalyst for dramatic and positive change. After release from inpatient care, outpatient psychological visits helped reinforce and maintain his improvements, while also helping to prevent his reentry into the subtle suicide zone.

Case Study: Cardiac Illness

Patricia is a middle-aged, married woman with two grown children. She worked for many years in the medical field and had a full and active life during her twenties and thirties. She was vibrant and happy during most of her early adult years. Things started to change when Patricia's mother died at a relatively young age due to side effects from cholesterol-lowering medications. The mother had suffered from a variety of cardiac problems, and Patricia soon discovered that she had similar genetic risks. She barely survived a massive heart attack in her early forties. She had bypass surgery, but developed chronic neck and back pain afterward because of the extraordinary efforts to save her life when she suffered the heart attack.

Immediately after her bypass surgery, Patricia became depressed, which is quite common. She fought through the depression, however. She began exercise and diet routines that made her the picture of physical health, and for a time she looked and felt better than she had in many years. Unfortunately, her good health did not last long because, like her mother, her body suffered painful side effects from the prescribed cholesterol medication. Mostly, she had excruciating leg cramps that lasted up to an hour. Her leg cramping became so painful and frequent at times that she felt she had no other choice but to stop the medications, at least for a while. Desperate, Patricia would periodically avoid taking her medication for a week or so to get some relief before resuming the medicine. She knew she was gambling with the possibility of another heart attack or stroke, but she also knew that her mother had died from a blood disorder caused by similar medications.

Over the decade or so after her heart attack, Patricia developed a severe case of rheumatoid arthritis and fibromyalgia. She never returned to her career in the medical field for any sustained period and now receives Social Security disability payments. As she puts it, "I have essentially been housebound since my heart attack." Presently, her husband and kids are very supportive, but Patricia feels there is little left in her life that she can do for enjoyment. She feels like a burden to her family and laments, "I'm half a wife." She has tried many different psychiatric medications and received some relief from the anti-anxiety medications Xanax and Klonopin. Unfortunately, however, she can no longer exercise, and although she watches what she eats, substantial weight gain has demoralized her.

Patricia's bypass surgery involved vein grafts for her heart, which her doctors say are only good for about ten years. They now say she needs surgery so that the grafts can be replaced and perhaps other defects addressed. However, Patricia not only refuses to consider another surgery but will not undergo any other invasive technique or even a stress test. The only procedure she will allow doctors to perform with respect to her heart is blood tests.

Is Patricia showing subtle suicide behavior by her refusal to undergo the invasive medical procedures? The answer, of course, is not a simple one. It depends on one's perspective and judgment. Patricia's case is similar to others we have seen, such as a prisoner who asks for execution because he doesn't want to live out a life sentence. How about people who commit "suicide by cop" or who refuse lifesaving medications or seek doctor-assisted suicide? Do these people fit the profile of subtle suicide?

In Patricia's case, we can argue that she is not doing anything actively self-destructive. She hasn't tried to kill herself and is not preoccupied with suicide per se. Moreover, she tries to minimize her pain experiences. On the other hand, she is unwilling to go through surgery to extend her life and says her family would be much better off if she died. She has no plan to commit overt suicide, but is candid in saying that dying in an accident or by natural means would be just fine with her. She does not care about living any longer because she doesn't have much to look forward to, no longer feels productive, is in pain and discomfort most of the time, and has to live with the uncertainty of what will happen in the future. With respect to the last point, she has significant financial worries and is horrified by the thought that she could suffer some sort of debilitating heart attack or stroke, creating a more disabling or even vegetative state.

Looking at Patricia's "big picture," we would say that she does suffer from subtle suicide. There is a part of her that wants to live and enjoy life, but that part isn't as strong as her desire to die. Thus, she is ambivalent about living, but the death wish is stronger than her life force. In the final analysis, therefore, Patricia is not willing to receive lifesaving measures. She is overwhelmed with feelings of helplessness and hopelessness, one of the living dead. She has little zest for life, enjoys very few activities or people, and is simply not focused on living. Her primary focus is on death, and how and when it will occur. These are hallmarks of the subtle suicide zone. Family members and health-care professionals have confronted her about her wish to avoid heart surgery, but she refuses to change her mind. She simply refuses to allow any invasive measures to extend her life.

On the positive side, Patricia has continued her psychotherapy on a regular basis. The counseling relationship gives her a safe, confidential place to get some emotional support and clarification of her thoughts and emotions. She doesn't really want to talk with family and friends about her innermost conflicts and feelings, because she doesn't want to burden them with her psychological and physical pain.

It is clear that she is more concerned about dying with dignity than with living as long as possible. Patricia doesn't feel she has any quality of life at this point, and there are many people in her life who do not understand her perspectives and values with respect to refusing another heart surgery. Although counseling sessions are not likely to get her out of her medically induced subtle suicide state, at least the sessions can help her feel better understood and supported.

Case Study: Sudden Impact of a Stroke

Andrew's case is another example of how a medical condition can push someone into the subtle suicide zone. Andrew worked into his sixties. One day at work, however, he suffered a stroke, which left him paralyzed on

one side of his body. Time and rehabilitation helped restore some movement, but during his rehabilitation at a hospital, he began to develop
"uncomfortable feelings" in his head that are hard to describe. He simply
says he has cloudy, dizzy sensations on a constant basis, like he is continuously drunk, although without the pleasant effects of alcohol intoxication.
These distressing sensations make it extremely hard for Andrew to concentrate. He had to retire from work early, something he never intended to
do. As he said in psychotherapy, "I loved my job. It was my life." As a
matter of fact, he says his wish was "to die on the job." At one point in
therapy, he blurted out that he wished the stroke had killed him.

Without work, Andrew suddenly found himself with little purpose left
in his life, and he began to drift into the subtle suicide zone. Now, his only
major purpose in life is to live long enough to see his malpractice case
against the hospital where he was receiving treatment after the stroke
come to a successful conclusion. He is sure that errors made at the hospital are responsible for the strange feelings in his head (and the facts seem
to support his belief). Winning his personal injury case would help provide
financial security for his wife and children. He also hopes that by winning
the case, there will be less chance that another patient will have to suffer
like he has for the mistakes made in his poststroke treatment.

Unfortunately, Andrew doesn't see any purpose for living beyond the
legal case. He always saw his role in life as financial provider for his family, and it was this role that was the foundation for his self-esteem in
adulthood. The stroke substantially and irreversibly altered his life overnight, and he can't imagine life ever being worthwhile again. He has
become a very angry man who takes a lot of his frustration out on whomever he is near. Antidepressant medication has helped somewhat with
respect to controlling his anger, but it hasn't touched the depth of his ambivalence about living and, more generally, his state of subtle suicide.

The challenge for Andrew in psychotherapy is to find some purpose in
life, something that will encourage him to live out the rest of his natural
life. If he cannot find any reason to live, he may not be able to endure the
pain of living and will be at high risk for overt suicide. At the very best,
he will continue a miserable life in the subtle suicide zone.

SUMMARY

We believe subtle suicide is quite common, and cases like those we have
just described are typical of many clients in counseling. Most of our case
study sufferers were well on their way to subtle suicide before they even
had the ability to fight it. The subtle suicide process is usually slow and
occurs without conscious awareness on the part of the victim. Some of
those we analyzed seemed to have had a subtle suicide process that was
dormant for many years before it appeared, like a cancer moving into

advanced stages. Usually, advancement of the subtle suicide process into a crisis stage seemed to be stimulated by some external pressure, like a relationship loss or breakup, job loss, deterioration in physical functioning, or traumatic experience. Whereas most respond to these types of stressors in constructive ways, the subtle suicide victim appears to be predisposed to destructive styles of coping. Shame, low self-esteem, and a tendency to turn anger inward are just some of the common factors that lead the victims to avoid, quit, and express aggression and/or neglect toward themselves. This process worsens life situations while weakening the will to live.

Our case studies suggest that the subtle suicide process often gets stronger in middle age and beyond. It is clear, however, that the seeds of the process are often planted early in life, even during the preteen years. We believe there are many people who defeat the subtle suicide condition at a relatively young age before it can develop fully. Our experience with family, friends, coworkers, and outpatients is consistent with this conclusion. Factors that appear to protect someone from subtle suicide tendencies are:

1. Having a positive social support system
2. Feeling competent to meet challenges
3. Developing a sense of purpose and meaning in life
4. Being able to have intimate connections with others
5. Feeling hopeful about living and the future
6. Having a generally positive self-concept
7. Being relatively free from intense physical pain and psychological trauma

Clinical experience shows us that people who become subtly suicidal as the result of physical disabilities differ from those whose origins are psychological. It seems that the former are more likely to be consciously aware of the onset and causes of their condition, which often appear quickly. Also, victims with physical disabilities are likely to see themselves as less responsible for their condition. On the other hand, subtle suicide victims who have a history of poor coping and avoidance behaviors tend to experience guilt over their personal inadequacies; consequently, they direct anger inward and develop self-punishing behaviors. If they get serious medical problems and physical discomforts as a result of these behaviors, they tend to accept these conditions as appropriate consequences of their irresponsible behavior. Because of the different dynamics between victims who become subtly suicidal as the result of a physical disability and those who have core psychological handicaps, it seems appropriate to ask if different treatment strategies should be used in each case. There are presently not enough clinical data to answer this question.

There are many different roots to subtle suicide. We are talking about a very complex process. Although many of the people in our case studies experienced a good deal of suicidal ideation, few actually attempted suicide. For varied reasons, most of them could not "pull the trigger." However, they were often able to engage in actions (excessive smoking, drinking, drug use, avoiding medical treatment, etc.) that could shorten or end their lives, making their impending death look like the result of natural causes.

In spite of many differences, our cases show several common themes. The subtle suicide victims suffered from similar cognitive and emotional experiences: shame, guilt, low self-esteem, depression, and self-hatred. Anger was expressed mainly as self-loathing, rather than being directed onto others. Also, shame seemed to operate in a way that not only lowered self-esteem but also made it very difficult for sufferers to express emotional pain and get needed help. Depression made it hard for victims to care enough about themselves to work consistently on bettering their lives.

Finally, we can say that when confronted with the subtle suicide process, those who demonstrated persistence in their therapies and who had positive support systems tended to fare best. This fact supports the idea that certain "protectors" can reduce the impact of negative factors, while other factors can act as "potentiators" of the condition. Furthermore, we can say with considerable confidence that making clients aware of the concept of subtle suicide and their tendencies in that direction helped them feel better understood and less alienated in their pain. Their awareness helped them ask some fundamental questions and form more positive thoughts about how their behaviors could turn their lives around in a better direction. Examples of such questions are:

- "Do I really want to kill myself slowly?"
- "Is this really any different than suddenly committing suicide?"
- "If I don't stop doing these things to myself, will I get into a position from which I can never return?"
- "Is my lack of progress due to my ambivalence about living, as opposed to medication or therapeutic ineffectiveness?"
- "If I stop hating myself and put positive energy into living, can I get out of the subtle suicide zone?"
- "Do I still have something to offer others?"
- "Do those close to me deserve a better effort on my behalf?"
- "Do I want to be remembered as someone who gave up on life?"

Chapter 4

Perspectives from Others: Case Studies

The effects of subtle suicide act like an infectious disease, spreading destructive influences to others like a contagion. To illustrate this process, we present a variety of case studies from the perspective of family members who must cope with a subtle suicide victim. We believe these cases illustrate many of the common destructive side effects of subtle suicide on significant others.

SUBTLE SUICIDE'S EFFECTS ON OTHERS

Case Study: Death Anxiety

We have all seen people defy or challenge death. We read or hear about people who jump out of airplanes, drive cars at frightening speeds, or work in organizations that require them to carry and perhaps use a gun. Many of us know of people who drink or drug themselves until they are unconscious or who refuse to take lifesaving medications properly. All these behaviors challenge death. Some are risking their lives in the service of other people, but others do so by reckless driving, wrist cutting, or drug overdosing, all for no apparent productive reason. It is certainly true that some who endanger their lives may be asking for help. Without knowing the dynamics of the individuals involved, however, it is hard to determine the motives behind death-defying risks.

For example, what would be the motivating factors in tightrope walker Karl Wallenda's fall to his death on a windy day in Puerto Rico? He chose to perform a high-wire act between two tall buildings without any net below. He didn't have to risk his life. At the very least, he could have chosen a more favorable day to perform. At the time of his stunt, he was around seventy years of age and had little, if anything, to prove professionally. He had been performing death-defying feats for decades. Was he challenging death? Did he want to die? Or did he simply want to "go out his way"? Was he subtly suicidal? After all, he had previously lost several members of the Wallenda family through horrible high-wire accidents. We will never know the answers to these questions, but these are the types of questions we need to learn more about, particularly as they relate to the subtle suicide process.

Ted is our case focus in this section. What we know about him was derived from intensive interviews with his parents. He is a thirty-year-old alcoholic who regularly challenges death in self-destructive manners. His upbringing was unremarkable. He was the older of two children, and his parents worked full-time. Throughout childhood, his academic record in school was exceptional, and he was a relatively well-rounded kid. He had many friends and liked sports.

Things began to fall apart for Ted in his early teens. A major turning point occurred with the death of a grandparent to whom he was extremely attached. A couple of years later, an uncle with whom he was also very close died. Shortly thereafter, he started skipping school. He missed about two months before his parents found out about the truancy. When they asked him why, he said, "Why should I go to school when I'm going to die anyway?"

During this time period, Ted also began to drink heavily and frequently. At fifteen, he drove cars around and had several accidents with family vehicles. Eventually, he was convicted of driving under the influence numerous times. Ted's parents had to save him from binges on many occasions. Typically, they found him in a drunken stupor in a dingy hotel room. Sometimes he had to be admitted to a hospital for alcohol poisoning and undergo detox. Incredibly, on several occasions his blood alcohol level registered over .40—five times the legal intoxication threshold in most states. He would ask about his blood levels upon exiting a comatose state and would be disappointed if he didn't set a new personal record!

Ted began puncturing his legs with a large syringe to inject animal steroids. He became very muscular and put huge, morbid, visible tattoos on his arms. He often drank alone and watched zombie-type movies endlessly. He idolized and read extensively about self-destructive icons like Anna Nicole Smith.

As he got older, Ted got some decent jobs, but couldn't keep them because of his heavy drinking. He got married and fathered a son, but this relationship was doomed from the start. After a divorce, his drinking worsened. He lost visitation rights, as did his parents despite their being very supportive of all concerned. Things came to a head when, in an alcoholic episode, he drove from his home state to a neighboring one and in the process stole a gun. When police tried to pull him over, Ted drove off at a high speed, and the police chased him. Fortunately, no one was killed. The police eventually overtook and arrested him, charging him with numerous offenses. When his parents showed up, he literally stunned them by saying, "I have now lived through one of my greatest challenges." His parents were grateful the police did not kill him. They even thanked them for not shooting their son. Obviously, Ted didn't feel the same; he was focused on how good it felt to challenge and survive death one more time.

Ted overwhelmed his parents for a long period of time, and they have required counseling for both their stress levels and marital problems that have ensued. Understandably, they often blame one another and displace their negative emotions on their partner. Also, they suffer from indecisiveness on how to handle the myriad of no-win situations they are presented with. One of their daughters has also suffered greatly. She wrote the following account of her feelings.

I didn't think any more pain would be caused to me by someone who was close to me. After being fired and cast aside by my "friends," I became extremely selective about who I let close to me. I did this to avoid any more heartache by those that I cared about. I never imagined the amount of betrayal that would inevitably come from my own blood, my brother. How I didn't see this coming is surprising given the history of his life. Yet, I still took for granted the fact that he would care enough about me to not cause me pain. I was very wrong.

For years, I've forgiven him. Over and over and over again I never faulted him for anything. I even continued to look up to him in some ways. That eventually faded, but not as quickly as one might have thought. Every important event in my life was never fully appreciated because of him. Yet I forgave him. Actually, I never even got angry at him for it; the whole time I just wanted to know that he was okay. When he destroyed my college graduation by disappearing and causing my parents severe stress and grief, I never once felt anger toward him, only concern. I'm not sure if he was on a drinking binge during my high school graduation but I know he wasn't there. I forgave him when he was fifteen, sixteen, and he drove me to and from school so intoxicated and so violently that I feared for my life every moment I was in the truck. I forgave him the numerous times I came home to an empty house and a suicide note left for me to read since he knew my parents wouldn't be home when I got home from school. It would make me believe he really went through with it, until he wrote them so often I eventually became numb to the words. I forgave him the one and only time I took his precious alcohol bottle (Wild Turkey) from him and went to pour it down the drain and looked at him just before doing so and saw for the first time in my life a look in his eyes I never recognized. It looked like a different person altogether; someone who had hurt me and did not feel remorse. I still forgave him but I now began to fear him. I forgave him the thousands of times I had to help heal the hurt he caused my parents. He would go off on a binge and I would be at home trying to remind my parents it wasn't each other they were mad at, but the alcohol. Notice I said alcohol and not his name. That's what we've always blamed it on. The fault lied with the alcohol, drugs, or even society for allowing such evils to be produced, but never with him. After years and years of this, he would become partially to blame but never fully responsible, but that is what love will do to ease the pain. It will make you angry with abstract or tangible things rather than the person you love. It's just easier that way. I forgave him when he stole my car while I was sleeping and threw up in it in the hot summer months when the smell painted the interior and wouldn't go away. Finally, I forgave him any responsibilities of being an older brother to me. I had to help him. Clean up after him, buy him food, give him money, car rides, etc. I didn't even do this as often as my parents or grandmother. I was simply one of a string of puppets he carried around that jumped when he plucked the right chord and I still never felt anger towards him.

In the past few months he was like a tornado that kept getting stronger and stronger and would rise up just when we thought the sky was clear. He nearly destroyed my parents in many ways; their relationship with each other and themselves. He ruined the rental house that my father worked so hard to rebuild after he damaged it the first time. He introduced me to thieves and dangerous drug dealers and put me in harm's way. He even let those people steal from me. He sold off any piece of furniture or personal belongings of mine that he could move. I even forgave him for this. But after the madness ended and we were cleaning up the debris of this tornado, something angered me. I first found out he was planning to sell my bed. I can only assume he would have sold my bedroom set if it wasn't so heavy to move. That was paid for by the last bit of my money I had in my account and I no longer had an income. I know it is only a material possession, but to me it represents the last thing or rather only thing I gained from my employment and he would have sold it. My employer took everything else away from me: my pride, my self-esteem, my friends, my income, my career, my house, my life. That bedroom set was the only thing left from my job and my brother would have sold it if it was possible. That, for some reason, hurt more than anything he had done to me or my family over the past fifteen years. Then I found out he sold my computer. That PC was like a diary of my life from the time I got it until about two years ago. I had personal documents on there, pictures, music, files from my college, my computer degrees, electronic receipts, everything, and he sold it to some low-life drug dealer who now knows all about me. That is just one hill too high for me to climb; so I just don't know if I will ever get over this heap of betrayal he built. It would be easier to forgive and forget if he even bothered to just write the words "I'm sorry." But when I asked my parents if he said anything during their visit to him in jail, their reply was: "Yes, he said it had to be this way. He knows he was out of control and he needs to be in a place away from temptation so he can get his life back together." For the first time in my life I thought to myself, What about our lives, or the lives of all of those he destroyed? For the first time I got angry, not at the alcohol or alcoholism, or the drugs, or society, but at him. For the first time it became clear to me that he is not capable of truly caring about anyone else but himself. I thought I lost my brother years ago to alcohol and drugs, but now I know I lost him completely. If someone asks me when the last time was that he acted like a brother to me or to remember the last good memory I have of him that was genuine, I honestly cannot remember.

Throughout Ted's life, he received parental support (often excessively enabling), drug and alcohol rehabilitations, and psychiatric medications, all of which failed to help him. This failure is not surprising, because Ted had—and has—no motivation to change; after all, he does not care about living. His primary purpose in life is simply to challenge what is unbeatable: death. He is at high risk for dying prematurely because of his self-destructive actions. It appears that his only hope at this time is for his parents to "set him free" so he can finally live independently with the consequences of his own choices. This change, together with well-targeted confrontations by a skilled therapist, might help.

Ted needs to be challenged with regard to his subtle suicide process. He needs to develop an understanding of how he can more productively cope with what is actually his death anxiety. He is so terrified of death that he spends much of his time challenging it. Currently, he says that it is just a matter of time until he is back in prison. He is fascinated with shows like *Prison Break*. It seems he has found his next self-sabotaging challenge!

Certainly, there are those who would argue that this case study simply reflects that of an alcoholic. In other words, his apparent subtle suicide process is simply a manifestation of his alcoholic personality and the effects of alcohol on his judgment and behaviors. Yes, alcohol can have profound effects on moods and thoughts and can lead to self-destructive behaviors, but we think there is more to Ted. First of all, there are many alcoholics who do not show Ted's severe patterns of self-destructiveness and risk-taking. Additionally, many alcoholics respond to treatment in much more favorable ways than Ted. Also, there was a quick onset of Ted's difficulties following the deaths of his grandfather and uncle. Furthermore, he was very consistent during his teenage and young adult years with respect to challenging death. Also, the key comments he made regarding his relationship with death were made while sober. Finally, being imprisoned has not led to significant changes in his attitudes.

Whatever the particular dynamics of Ted's case, it is clear that his subtle suicide patterns swept up his parents like a raging flood. His actions put them in a very difficult position. On the one hand, in their hearts they wanted to be supportive and loving parents and to nurture Ted through the hard times. On the other hand, in their heads they knew they should be tough on Ted and allow him to face the negative consequences of his actions. This dilemma is one most parents face at some level, although thankfully not at the level that confronted Ted's parents. The level of guilt and the questions that parents ask themselves in these types of situations ("What could we have done differently?") often cause a great deal of suffering.

Case Study: The Dissociative Spouse

Carina was sexually and physically abused by her father and emotionally and physically abused by her mother. Numerous psychological problems developed, including what some doctors diagnosed as a form of dissociative disorder (multiple personality). In extreme cases of dissociative disorder, the individual's conscious awareness in the present becomes dissociated (split or separated) from previous memories and thoughts. The condition can involve memory loss, problems in establishing a firm and consistent identity, and even displays of separate personalities (a Jekyll-and-Hyde type of separation).

Carina was raised in an extremely dysfunctional family with little intimacy and communication among family members. Both parents abused alcohol. She married at a relatively young age and had children. Her husband, Al, worked, but she could not sustain gainful employment. Over the years, Al felt the need to take on more and more financial and other responsibilities. Many arguments took place because of financial problems, arguments the children observed and became involved in.

Carina was very treatment resistant. Hospitalizations, many psychiatric medications, and numerous doctors did not produce any significant change. The medications often seemed to make the situation worse by producing a drowsy numbness resulting in a zombie-like approach to life. Eventually, a variety of physical problems developed, including obesity, thyroid imbalance, arthritis, and breathing difficulties from smoking. Depression and social withdrawal increased over time, and unfortunately a subtle suicide process developed. There was a slow regression downward over a long period of time that put Carina in the subtle suicide zone, caring little about life or self, which was poorly defined to begin with.

What effects did the subtle suicide spouse have on the children? Both children have been treated for psychological problems; one of them also shows strong subtle suicide patterns (remember the effects of modeling we noted earlier). This offspring has been psychiatrically hospitalized more than once, has made suicidal gestures, and shows minimal self-care, motivation, or self-respect. This adult child shows direct influence from the subtle suicide parent.

What effects did Carina have on Al? Al has been extremely frustrated for several decades and has tried many approaches to help with Carina's suffering and the family dysfunctions. Nothing has worked. It has been excruciatingly difficult for our client to live with someone who does not care about life. Living with a self-centered spouse with little to give has proven to be very depressing and has taken a great toll on our client, who has worked a lot of overtime, given up hobbies, lost thousands of hours of sleep, and been treated for depression for many years.

The chronic subtle suicide victim is particularly harmful toward others, although not in deliberate fashion, because the sufferer's style of life is so hopeless and helpless. The victim does not care about life enough to take persistent efforts toward constructive change. As a result, family members and friends have little choice but to protect themselves emotionally by keeping their distance. Sadly, that reaction only further alienates and frustrates all concerned and puts additional stress on the relatives and friends of the sufferer.

Case Study: The Accident at Work

This case is told from the perspective of Emily, a client in therapy, and concerns her father, Trevor, who developed into a subtle suicide victim following an accident at work. Trevor grew up with twelve siblings. His mother was an alcoholic, and his father was psychologically unstable and had several long-term psychiatric hospitalizations. His formative years obviously presented risks for later problems, but he got through that period, and his early adulthood seemed typical. He married and had several children. To make ends meet, he typically worked two jobs and often put in about eighty hours a week. He enjoyed his work and took pride in knowing he was a good provider, though his schedule took a toll on the marriage, often leading to arguments with his wife.

In his mid-forties, Trevor's life drastically changed in one instant. While walking backwards and guiding equipment at work, he fell into a hole that should have been covered. He suffered serious and permanent back injuries and could not return to work. A friend offered to build a workshop in Trevor's cellar so he could have a part-time business and make some extra money, but he wasn't interested. Trevor went from working eighty hours a week to zero, a change that challenged the whole family emotionally and financially. He also suffered chronic pain and was angry at his company to the point where he threatened legal action.

Trevor slowly spiraled downward. He slept excessively and spent hours staring motionless out a window or at the television screen. As Emily reports: "Throughout the years, my sisters and I basically grew up without a father. Oh, he was our dad and he loved us all, but his state of mind never allowed any type of bond to develop between any of us. In fact, our roles were almost reversed, and for years, it was actually *us* who reprimanded *him!* Often, my father would snap into some state where he became angry and sometimes violent without any warning. Other times, he became docile, almost childlike."

Trevor regularly ate foods that aggravated his diverticulitis, often requiring trips to the hospital. Even though diabetic, he ate foods high in sugar and refused to follow recommendations to walk to help his heart condition. The fact that he had a pacemaker did not seem to motivate him in any positive way. He also has weak hearing, but seldom wears his two hearing aids.

Trevor was psychiatrically hospitalized more than once for depression and anger management problems. He has been on psychiatric medications ever since the accident and has been treated extensively by a psychiatrist and psychologist. The benefits of such treatments have been minimal. He has minimal motivation to take more positive steps in his life. In fact, it seems the only thing that Trevor cares about is buying lottery tickets. He frequently talks about how he will give the winnings away to his children and wife.

Since the accident, Trevor's wife has been the family breadwinner and primary caregiver at home. Emily believes the strains on her mother have caused her to become resentful and made her aggressive toward everyone at home. Her behavior has produced a lot of emotional distance between her and the children. The children, on the other hand, have remained relatively close to one another emotionally. It seems they have bonded in reaction to their common psychological pain. Emily, however, is aware of the psychological costs of her family situation:

"Growing up I often felt melancholy, insecure, unloved, shy, and having no self-esteem. Today, I still have difficulty with relationships because it is hard for me to trust others. I believe that I am selfish and overemotional. I feel things too deeply and I think too intensely. I am easily consumed and saddened by both personal and worldly events surrounding me. And while I can say that I love my father, we share little or no relationship. I often look at my dad with a heavy heart. I love him for the sacrifices he had every intention of making for my family, and I can't help but see inside of him all the tribulation he has gone through. Sometimes he wakes up in the morning, sits in his chair, and stares out the glass door for hours with tears in his eyes. Sometimes he gets violent and lurches towards one of my sisters' throats. In an instant, his anger is turned on as quickly as a light switch. Sometimes he's like a little child rather than a father. He is gentle, innocent, and vulnerable. I know since the loss of his job so many years ago, the feeling that 'a man isn't a real man if he can't support his family' continually haunts him. The very notion kills him. Or perhaps in a strange way ... he is just killing himself."

Trevor's situation is not simply a case of job loss and depression. There is a complex interaction of subtle suicide effects on a family structure. Trevor has given up on himself and life; he has stopped caring about living, and his helplessness and hopelessness have affected his wife and children in various and negative ways. His subtle suicide coping style has affected the whole family, making things much more difficult than need be. To one degree or another, Trevor caused everyone in his household to feel frustrated, depressed, and rejected. As a result, Emily sought therapy, and her siblings suffered emotionally.

It is clear to us that children of subtle suicide victims need to be watched closely for psychological problems. It is extremely stressful to live with the subtly suicidal person. Sufferers may not kill themselves, but the quality of their lives is lowered significantly and the subtle suicide process is almost guaranteed to impact heavily on significant others. The degree of impact on children will depend on:

1. The age of the child at the onset of the parent's subtle suicide
2. The intensity and length of the subtle suicide process
3. The presence of other siblings
4. The quality of the relationship with the parent before becoming subtly suicidal
5. The child's gender (same or opposite sex as parent)
6. The general emotional stability of the child
7. How well the other parent or caretakers can adapt to the sufferer's condition

FAMILY MEMBERS' REACTIONS

In the next chapter, we will provide more specific advice for family members of the subtle suicide victim. For now, we want to end this discussion with some general considerations. Our case studies show how family members of subtle suicide victims suffer psychologically. Our clients typically come to us on psychotropic medication prescribed by their family doctor or a psychiatrist. They often are suffering from physical ailments, complain about missing significant time from work, and describe how relationships with friends and neighbors have fallen apart. Whether we're talking about parents, spouses, or siblings, those who are close to a subtle suicide victim have given countless hours of time and energy, and often spent considerable sums of money, to help their loved one. They also mourn the absence of any genuine relationship with the victim, who usually has become a shell of a person. Acknowledging this reality is extremely demoralizing, because they see few options when living with someone who consistently acts in depressive, careless, hopeless, and abusive ways.

Our experience tells us that family members often follow one of three roads when they deal with subtle suicide victims. First, they can try to change the subtle suicide victim. However, because they don't have direct control over the victim, this option typically fails. People will only change in our preferred direction if they have sufficient motivation to do so, and as we have seen, subtle suicide victims seldom have enough of this sort of motivation. Second, the family can get depressed, angry, and hopeless along with the victim. This reaction is kind of an "If you can't beat them, join them" response. It is interesting that some families seem to follow that road, and the subtle suicide pattern runs through the family like a virus. From a therapeutic and practical perspective, of course, this is a relatively poor alternative. Finally, family members can distance themselves from the victim—physically, emotionally, or both. Coworkers and counselors can manage this alternative fairly easily, and sometimes even siblings and spouses can do so. Parents, however, tend to be another story. Victims turn to parents more frequently for help, and parents also feel the most responsibility and unconditional love toward the victim. We saw in Ted's case how excruciatingly difficult it can be for parents to turn their backs on their children, even when others are begging them to stop the enabling process and they have done everything possible to deter their child's self-destructive actions. It is also true, of course, that children have a very difficult time distancing themselves from a parent who suffers from the subtle suicide condition.

No matter who the family member might be, relatives of the subtle suicide victim are very vulnerable to depression and other psychological disorders. The high levels of stress that result from being around the victim can be overwhelming. Sleepless nights, excessive worry, public embarrassment and shame, loss of money due to legal entanglements and theft, anger over broken promises and lies, frustration and resentment relating to taking care of someone else's responsibilities, and feelings of hopelessness with respect to the unchanging situation are just some of the types of stressors involved.

Family members of the subtle suicide victim are quite vulnerable to what psychologists call *learned helplessness*. This condition can develop when people come to believe that there is nothing they can do to stop unpleasant events from impacting on them. Parents of the subtle suicide victim often find themselves in a sort of "damned if you do, damned if you don't" situation. As a result, they may eventually give up on the victim, while also becoming more passive and helpless in other areas of their lives. This is an extremely dangerous point to reach, and parents and loved ones must resist going down this road. They need to stop taking responsibility for the subtle suicide victim's decisions and actions, and stop feeling so helpless. Their attitude must be: "We need to accept that we are not damned if we do and damned if we don't. We are damned if we *do too much!*"

The time eventually comes when, after repeated attempts to produce positive change in a subtle suicide victim have failed, it is time for the family to say, "We have been beating our heads against the wall too long, and it's time to stop." The family can still be supportive, by encouraging the victim to get needed medical and psychological help and continuing to be good listeners. These strategies, however, should not include taking responsibility for the victim's problems or enabling them through inappropriate attention, sympathy, approval, or help. Such enabling will help maintain the self-defeating and self-destructive patterns.

There are many negative emotional experiences for family members that occur naturally when coping with the subtly suicidal. These people can exasperate and anger those around them with their self-defeating and self-destructive behavior patterns. They instill anxiety in those around them with their neglectful, careless, and dangerous behaviors, not to mention their comments like: "I really don't care whether I wake up tomorrow," "Life is meaningless," "You would be better off without me," "I should never have been born," or "I live for today because I don't see a tomorrow." Obviously, living with someone who talks and acts in these ways is very difficult. Generally, the more intimate the relationship, the more demoralizing the effects, which is why parents, spouses, and children are usually the most affected by the subtly suicidal person.

The human costs of subtle suicide are huge. It is next to impossible to have a decent marriage and family life while living with a subtle suicide sufferer. The "I don't care" attitude, self-defeating behaviors, and reckless acts can make things difficult and even dangerous for all involved, causing "accidents" that change or ruin lives and costing society billions of dollars in mental health, drug and alcohol, and medical treatment. When intervention and rehabilitation services work, it all seems worthwhile. However, all too often the subtle suicide condition is not identified early and is left to fester until the prognosis is unfavorable.

_____ *Chapter 5* _____

Getting and Giving Help

How do we help someone who is intensely and chronically ambivalent about living? What can you as a parent, spouse, sibling, child, or friend do for the subtle suicide victim? The task is hard, because it's like trying to feed someone who isn't sure about wanting to eat, or complimenting someone who hates such attention. We all know that if we try to force-feed foods or compliments to someone, what we force in is likely to be spit out. Thus, the issue becomes how we move in a sensitive way through the helping process, and in such a way that the victim sees our comments and intentions as genuine and acceptable. Equally important, we want to feel that our efforts have a chance at being effective.

In this chapter, we will discuss strategies and techniques anyone can use in helping subtle suicide victims and getting them appropriate professional help. In some cases, these approaches may also be helpful in preventing someone who is showing signs of subtle suicide from entering the subtle suicide zone. We may fail, but at least we will know we have done everything in our power to help.

Before beginning our discussion, we need to admit something that acquaintances of some suicidal victims find very difficult to face: some victims—a small percentage—have made a choice to enter and remain in the subtle suicide zone. They have resigned themselves to this life. For instance, they may be in chronic and extreme pain and have decided they have little purpose left in life and nothing significant to look forward to. In this type of case, it may very well be that our only reasonable option is to accept that there is nothing we can do to help them get out of the subtle suicide zone. Certainly, subtle suicide victims have the right to live with the consequences of their own choices, even if we don't understand or agree with them.

Fortunately, we find that most people in the subtle suicide zone *do* want to get out and, with some motivation and effort, can do so. Typically, though, they need a big push, because they are often not capable of mustering the motivation to pull themselves out. They may need considerable help from those around them. In the sections that follow, we discuss what we consider to be the primary tasks in helping the subtle suicide victim.

A REVIEW OF CHOICES FACING FAMILY

At the end of chapter 4, we listed three paths family and friends of the subtle suicide victim often choose to take. Let's review them before we get into more specifics.

1. They can try to change the victim. As we noted, this choice typically fails. We are often dealing with an adult who has years of personality and behavior development behind them, and their basic personality traits are fairly fixed. If family and friends try to mold the victim into their image of what that person should be, they are probably going to be frustrated every step of the way.
2. They can spiral downward along with the victim and allow the victim to take them along into emotional states of depression, despair, anger, and anxiety. Obviously, this path is not a good one, with the subtle suicide condition spreading like a contagious disease.
3. They can emotionally and physically distance themselves from the victim. Unfortunately, this choice is easier said than done. Asking parents, for instance, to disown a son or daughter in the hopes of shocking them out of their subtle suicide spiral may be an unreasonable request. Still, many families attempt this step, but find that the consequences are not helpful and may damage them as much as the victim.

Families, friends, and colleagues should avoid the three choices above as much as possible—especially the first two. Each comes with a high risk of failure. That being said, we do believe there are proactive, productive, loving, and supportive steps families and others can take to help the subtle suicide victim. Those steps, however, should take place within a certain context and without sacrificing the individuality, stability, and independence of the helpers. Let's now summarize what we have found to be the best ways to go about helping our sufferers.

Recognize the Victim

We have covered many case examples in the previous chapters, and there are some common themes in subtle suicide cases. Most victims:

- Have little purpose or meaning in their lives
- Have difficulty establishing and maintaining intimate relationships

- Believe they have few friends to give them needed social support (sometimes this belief is correct, but not always)
- Don't show much awareness of their subtle suicide condition, and show little insight into important issues, conflicts, and fears in their lives
- Have a deep sense of ambivalence about living
- Show weak motivation to persist in efforts at positive living
- Suffer intense emotional conflicts involving shame, guilt, anger, depression, and so forth
- Are pessimistic and hopeless about life
- Do not believe, or act like, they can master their lives better by controlling their thoughts and actions

Obviously, these symptoms will appear to different degrees in different victims. The fact remains, however, that loved ones are going to have a difficult time challenging and reducing these symptoms. Still, just because the task is hard should not stop us from trying to intervene. In many cases, significant others can satisfy, at least partially, some of the wants and needs of the victim. Furthermore, these efforts can help supplement more formal treatment by trained and experienced professionals.

In the appendix at the end of this book, we provide a brief questionnaire that can help in determining one's leanings in the direction of subtle suicide. This survey is not intended to serve as a formal diagnostic instrument, and scores should not be interpreted as indicating a subtle suicide condition. Getting the person you are concerned about to take this questionnaire, however, can be a first step. The individual may begin thinking about the possibility of a deeper problem than just some self-defeating actions that are present such as gambling or drug and alcohol abuse. Also, the questionnaire can be helpful in starting a dialogue and showing someone that you are concerned and want to reach out and help.

Take the First Steps of Intervention

We must assure victims that we care about them. Many people think that simply saying, "I really care about you, and that's why I'm worried about your behavior," should provide victims with enough support and encourage them to make an effort to get better. The fact is, however, that victims need to *see* we care about them, and the only way for that to happen is to show some caring actions to back up our words.

What sorts of actions are necessary?

- We need to listen to sufferers' comments without being critical or judgmental and without diagnosing them. In other words, we need to show we understand their point of view. The greatest obstacle to helping someone is saying: "You know what's wrong with you? Here's what's wrong with you...." Comments like this show we are approaching the problem from our own perspective and ignoring the perspective of the victim.

- We need to demonstrate to victims how important they are to us and what they mean to us. Again, we must do so by action more than by word. Supportive actions may help give sufferers purpose and meaning in their lives. We must do what is needed to help support them through these difficult times, including getting them the professional help they most likely need.

- We must remember that support for victims does not mean indulgence, enabling, or protecting them from the consequences of their inappropriate actions. We must place the responsibility for their behavior where it belongs: on their shoulders. After all, it is their life. We need to respect their choices even when we don't agree with those choices, while reminding them that they, not we, have to face the consequences of their behaviors.

- We need to avoid oversimplifying the situation by incorrectly attributing the subtle suicide condition to a disease, addiction, psychological disorder, or lack of willpower. In the case of subtle suicide, we need to help the sufferer face deeper core conflicts. If we focus only on symptoms, we will probably get superficial and temporary change at best.

- We need to resist the temptation to tell victims what they should or should not do, as in: "You've got to stop drinking! Can't you see you're killing yourself?" Being too forceful or direct can lead to stubbornness and rebellion, which is not desirable in these cases. Listeners see such comments as threats to their freedom to make personal choices. As a result, they tend to become more stubborn, rebellious, and resist making change, even if they know change is in their best interest.

How to Respond to Victims' Comments

As parents, spouses, children, siblings, and friends, we cannot expect to function as professional counselors. We must be realistic about what we can do. Given that caution, however, we should nevertheless believe that we can be helpful to subtle suicide individuals. So often, though—especially in the emotional context of most of our conversations with the victim—we just don't know what to say. We usually end up yelling, throwing our arms up in surrender, or simply turning and walking away. We can do better, and in this section we give some examples of typical kinds of comments that could be very helpful in conversation with the subtle suicide person.

As noted above, the temptation in conversations is to be quite directive, explaining what the victim is doing wrong, what the problem is, and the need for change. In effect, this strategy involves an evaluative response, in which we attempt to impose our will and values on another person. This approach rarely works, and we believe a more nondirective style is appropriate, especially as a beginning to intervention efforts. By *nondirective*, we mean a style in which we guide others toward recognizing and expressing their choices, rather than actively pointing out alternatives to them. Thus, there are key questions you can ask to help a victim think about potential choices, as well as to recognize some personal responsibility with this difficult condition.

We recommend this nondirective approach, although we recognize that more confrontational, challenging, and direct approaches may be appropriate in some cases, particularly severe ones. But there are risks involved in confrontational approaches, and ideally they should come only from a professional. In untrained hands, confrontational responses may make the subtle suicide victim more defensive and produce negative and unproductive reactions.

Comment: "There's nothing for me to live for any longer. I don't care whether I live or die."

Response: "We often need to change our purposes and goals as life goes by. You had meaning in life before, and you can once again develop purposeful activity at this point in your life. What do you think is holding you back?"

Comment: "I've tried therapy, I've tried medication. None of it works. I might as well give up. My life isn't ever going to be worth anything again."

Response: "Maybe you haven't had a therapist or medication that is effective for you. You haven't tried them all, right? Also, one thing is for sure, people in counseling need to work at it to see significant and positive change. Have you really been motivated to help yourself? Have you really given these methods a chance to work?"

Comment: "Life sucks! It's just too hard. I'll never be the type who commits suicide, but I don't care if I live another day."

Response: "I agree that life doesn't seem worth it at times. I imagine just about everyone has those feelings at one time or another. I know I have. But I also bet most people would say that life is what we make it. Life deals the hand, but we decide how we want to play it. Have you asked yourself what you're willing to face, what you need to do to get more out of your life? Do you think there are better choices you can make?"

Comment: "I can't get over things that happened a long time ago when I was a kid. These memories haunt me; I'm damaged forever. Some things we just can't overcome. It's just no use in trying. Life isn't worth living anymore. I've tried, but it's no use."

Response: "I guess we all have our crosses to bear. Lots of people have long-term problems dealing with traumatic things. You hear about them on the news all the time. But look at all the stories of people who have moved on and learned to cope with all kinds of traumas, injuries, even death. If they can do it, why can't you? I bet a lot of them got some counseling. Are you willing to give counseling a try before you throw in the towel? Isn't it at least an option?"

Comment: "I don't know why I hurt myself so much. Things go well for a while and then I do stupid things and hurt myself. It seems like I go three steps forward and four steps back. What is my problem?"

Response: "I guess we don't always know why we do what we do. That seems natural to me. But you're asking some pretty deep questions, and maybe if you see a counselor, you can get some answers about why you're so self-defeating and self-destructive. Maybe the answers will give you more desire to live. What do you think?"

Comment: "I don't know why I can't take my medications and go to therapy like I'm supposed to. I don't want to work or even get out of bed. It has been this way for a long time. I don't even care about my friends and family. Living isn't important to me."

Response: "Sounds logical to me. Why would you care about taking your medicine or going to doctors if you don't care about living? Until you care about living, you're sure not going to be doing much of anything that makes you feel good. You'll just keep giving yourself more pain. Is pain what you want, though? You have to decide, because you're the only one who can change your life. Only you can decide if you have a desire to live your life to the fullest."

Avoid Stereotyping the Victim

We need to remember that loved ones cannot be expected to function as formal counselors with subtle suicide victims. Getting the sufferer into counseling is an important goal, but sometimes not an easy one. First of all, subtle suicide victims usually do not care enough about their lives to enter into, much less stay in, therapy or to take needed psychiatric medications as prescribed. Second, they have often already been in unproductive therapy that frustrated and disappointed them. In spite of these hurdles, it is important to remember that subtle suicide victims need to know that loved ones think they are worth the effort.

Family members, friends, and others who have close contact with subtle suicide victims often misunderstand them. The sufferers typically appear to be stubborn and opposed to any suggestions others make. The problem develops when loved ones decide that the victims are being stubborn and resistant because they are fundamentally lazy and unmotivated. The fact is that the stubbornness and resistance should be seen as reactions to the subtle suicide condition. Yes, victims have quit life, so to speak, but there are reasons for their self-defeating approaches. If family members write them off as lazy and beyond hope, then the odds that they will never recover are greatly increased. Loved ones must remember that persistence is one of the keys to helping the subtle suicide victim.

Diagnostic Labels Are Not Solutions

Family members must guard against feeling relieved and reassured as soon as a loved one is diagnosed with a particular condition, such as bipolar disorder, clinical depression, addiction, or social anxiety. When one of these labels is put on someone, we have a tendency to think we have explained what is wrong and that steps may now be taken to produce a "cure." Diagnostic labels often make us feel too comfortable.

In the case of subtle suicide victims, these diagnoses can provide a false sense of security. First of all, the label may be downright wrong. Second, even if it is accurate, we may confuse what is cause and what is effect. For instance, suppose someone is labeled a compulsive gambler. We need to be careful in our analyses of cause and effect. Is the addiction the fundamental problem that is causing the subtle suicide profile, or is the addiction the result of the lack of desire to live (subtle suicide) that occurred because of the individual's life experiences and deeper core conflicts? Families must realize this very important distinction, because they may be mistakenly lulled into believing that the subtle suicide sufferer simply needs to stop drinking, gambling, or take psychiatric medicine in order to be "cured."

Do Not Depend on Psychiatric Medications

Psychiatric drugs can become part of the problem. Diagnoses like bipolar disorder, anxiety disorder, and depression have skyrocketed recently and are being applied to younger and younger clients. As a result, we have millions of people taking psychiatric medications. Although many people are helped considerably by these medications, are we really supposed to believe these medications will cure sufferers? Can a pill undo decades of psychological conflict? Are we also supposed to believe that all of a sudden we have this many people who need psychiatric medication just because the pharmaceutical companies have made them readily available? At best, medications given for anxiety, depression, and other psychological issues help reduce symptoms; they do not address key life conflicts or produce cures.

For the subtle suicide victim, families must realize that, in the vast majority of cases, the victim's core problems can best be targeted by psychological, not medicinal, intervention. As we pointed out earlier, some people will spontaneously improve without any professional help. They get better by using their own resources and coping actions, and they profit from having lots of social support. Others, however, need a great deal of help, and that help will probably go beyond psychiatric medication. We are not opposed to the use of medications to treat symptoms of depression, anxiety, post-traumatic stress, bipolar disorder, and the like. However, we strongly object to *depending on* these medications to address complex psychological phenomena, including the subtle suicide condition, especially as the sole intervention strategy.

Psychiatric medications treat symptoms, not problems. Sometimes they do not work at all, and on other occasions they make things worse. Worse yet, advertisements present the simplistic idea that psychological problems are biological and suggest that pills will magically change a deep and complex psychological condition. Rarely will this approach work. Certainly it is true that medications can often help get sufferers moving in a positive direction. Continued movement in that direction, however, usually requires psychological intervention and social support.

Find the Right Therapist

All counselors are not equal. Some will have a better chemistry with the sufferer, and some will be more understanding and effective with this difficult-to-treat condition. We recommend that families help get subtle suicide victims to professional counselors who will look at the "whole person." That is, we believe the most effective therapists for this condition are those who look at current symptoms and conflicts in the context of sufferers' life history; the development of their subtle suicide condition; their life purposes, goals, and values; and their support systems. Does the professional have to be versed in subtle suicide dynamics? Not necessarily. Should family members tell the counselor they think this is a case of subtle suicide? Not necessarily. We are just saying that it is vital to make sure that the subtle suicide victim is not treated in an overly simplistic or cookie-cutter fashion, with automatic emphasis on standard treatment of anxiety, depression, alcohol/drug abuse, and so on. In the case of subtle suicide, these are insufficient treatments.

Success Is Not Guaranteed

It is important to remember that not all subtle suicide victims can be treated successfully. This fact was clear in some of the case studies we reviewed. Thus, it is crucial to remind ourselves that we can only do so much and then to do the best we can. Even when we have put forth a good, sincere, and maximum effort on behalf of the victim, we need to let the chips fall where they may. Like the sufferer, as helpers we need to be committed to our purposes and values, but also to accept the limits of what we can change.

CASE STUDY: HELPING THE SUBTLE SUICIDE VICTIM

We think a recent case shows some of the important points we have been making about the positive role friends and family can play in helping the subtle suicide victim. This case concerns Justina, a young woman who worked very hard for many years to become a professional athlete. As is so often the case, however, things did not go according to plan. Even though Justina had fantastic athletic success in high school and college, following her graduation from college she was just not talented enough to qualify for a professional league in her sport. She managed to find a good job, but was not happy and found no personal fulfillment in her career. She became depressed and felt like she lacked a purpose in life.

Justina continued to have a stable relationship with a guy she had met in college, and they were living together quite happily when she became pregnant and had a baby. Still, as was the case with her job, Justina did not feel fulfilled. She didn't feel a part of a real family; something was missing. Suddenly, her behavior changed drastically: she stopped her exercise routine, something that had been a fundamental part of her life for years. At the same time, she began partying excessively, drinking more and more alcohol, experimenting with recreational drugs, and even abusing pain medications. Her family and friends were shocked and confused because they felt they no longer knew her. Slowly, Justina drifted away from them, descending into a different, more isolated world. She spoke to no one about her frustrations, her fears and anxiety about her future, and her depression over not realizing her athletic goals. More and more, she felt sorry for herself and acted in increasingly self-defeating ways through drug and alcohol abuse. Justina was in jeopardy of losing everything of value in her life, but she said she didn't care. She was standing right on the edge of the subtle suicide zone.

For a time, Justina was able to hide her excessive use of drugs and alcohol, but of course her partner eventually realized the extent of her problem, and he made sure other family members were aware of her issues. Many of them already knew things had changed with Justina, but the concerns of her mate brought a new sense of urgency to the situation. They proceeded to develop a plan of action to help her out of the downward spiral she was in.

The first phase of the plan was to make it clear to Justina that they loved her and wanted to help and support her. However, they were concerned and disappointed in her actions; she could not continue her behavior and expect any sort of enabling behavior on their part. They basically took a "tough love" approach to the problem, saying, "We're here for you, but you need to change, and that's that!"

Justina's family moved very forcefully to help her get into a residential drug and alcohol rehabilitation center. After one week, though, the program directors concluded that drugs and alcohol were not her core problem, and that she needed a different type of care. It is at this point that Justina was very fortunate. As we have said again and again, too often we look at the subtle suicide victim's symptoms (such as drug, alcohol, or gambling addictions) and decide they are the problem, when in fact these addictive actions usually represent deeper issues. Justina's professional caregivers decided that her addictions to drugs and alcohol were brought on by her use of these substances to self-medicate psychological pain. To us, *self-medicate* means "avoid." Justina was numbing—that is, avoiding—her pain of failure, frustration, and shame because she never became a professional athlete, along with a variety of other issues that surfaced as time went by.

Justina's therapy now switched from a focus on her addictions to individual psychotherapy and counseling to help her deal with more basic core negative emotions that were driving the addictions. She had to confront and deal with these negative emotions and stop avoiding them. Importantly, family help continued. Not only did they remain supportive as she continued her therapy, but they also insisted she live with close relatives as long as was necessary. They took very proactive, assertive steps to insure that she would no longer be able to associate with those people and places that were a part of her substance abuse world.

Family intervention in this case occurred well before Justina was fully involved in the subtle suicide zone. Still, the intervention illustrates some important principles:

- The family moved quickly and decisively.
- The family was supportive and helpful, yet they insisted on following through with appropriate professional help.
- The family was empathetic, not sympathetic. They did not feel sorry for Justina, but they showed an understanding of her negative emotions over falling short of her goals. They also made it clear that such understanding did not mean acceptance. The family would in no way accept or enable her self-defeating actions.
- The family was honest with Justina about how they felt and insisted she be equally honest with them. Their help was a two-way street. Their support was really support for Justina's efforts and motivation to reach a better understanding of her internal fears and to turn her life around.

Justina's case has an excellent prognosis. During psychotherapy, she saw more clearly the negative path she had begun to take and, more importantly, why she had moved down that road. She began to see that the relationship with her alcoholic father was important in causing her emotional problems. She had always longed for his approval, but never seemed able to accept the fact that his approval was virtually impossible to receive. When she was confronted with the reality that she would not be a professional athlete, she had neither the personal nor family resources to help her deal with the question, "Where do I go from here?"

As Justina gained some insight into her problems during therapy, she moved emotionally closer to her spouse's family (but not to her own father) and realized the strength of their love for her. She refocused her energies on positive goals and purposes and stopped being ruled by the disappointments of failing to realize old and outdated goals. In a nutshell, and most significantly, Justina stopped avoiding negative emotions and psychological pain; she accepted the facts that such things are a necessary part of life and that facing them is a vital part of personal growth and maturity. Finally, she faced her anger toward her father that she had suppressed with athletics and then with alcohol and drugs.

Justina learned to ask herself the fundamental question the subtle suicide victim must ask to begin climbing out of the subtle suicide zone: What am I avoiding? To continue the climb, the victim must then find the courage and strength to confront emotions found in the answer to that fundamental question. Family and friends can provide much in helping the victim to find that courage and strength.

Part II

Advanced Topics

Chapter 6

Theoretical and Historical Considerations

THEORETICAL VIEWS OF SUICIDE

The seminal works in psychology dealing with self-destructive behaviors are decades old, and we will review both their associated theories and more contemporary ones. We have chosen to cover only what we consider to be the major theoretical frameworks that apply, because it is impractical to attempt to cover all possibly relevant conceptualizations.

Psychodynamic Theory

Different psychodynamic approaches to self-destructive behavior share some common elements. They view self-destructive behavior as developing early in life, when our personalities are very immature. Thus, such behavior patterns represent underlying unconscious dynamics that are seen as primarily internal conflicts. The sufferer's actions are viewed as being caused by abnormal environmental circumstances early in life, but are sustained by internal conflicts, which are mostly unconscious.

Earlier theorists who wrote about suicide, such as Karl Menninger and Norman Farberow, organized their discussions around the effects of self-destructive motives. Menninger pioneered discussion of how some people were "accidents waiting to happen," neglecting their physical well-being and generally living neurotic lives filled with anxiety. These discussions came at a time when psychodynamic approaches were dominant in psychology, and this theme was the focus of causes of abnormal psychology.

The first attempt to comprehensively address topics related to subtle suicide is found in Menninger's classic work, *Man against Himself* (1938), in which he outlined a psychoanalytic approach to self-destruction. Simply put, Menninger postulated that self-destructive acts are caused by an imbalance between our unconscious life and death instincts. This imbalance creates a situation where the ego cannot control the death instincts, thereby setting the stage for uncontrolled aggression to occur. This type of regression can be manifested against oneself or others. Presumably, when the superego is relatively well developed, individuals are more likely to turn aggression toward themselves, as they suffer too much guilt to consciously hurt others. Theoretically speaking, people of this type can develop a propensity to be passively self-destructive. Conversely, a weak superego leads to hostility displaced onto others because of a poorly developed conscience.

Attachment Theory

Harry Harlow's research with monkeys changed how we think about human needs. His experiments dramatically demonstrated our fundamental need for love, particularly in the early stages of life. Harlow showed that monkeys deprived of contact with their mothers or other family members from birth, for a month or more, suffered serious and sometimes lifelong negative effects on their development. He showed that it was not unusual for these monkeys to self-mutilate by biting or scratching themselves or ripping out their own fur. Typically, emotionally deprived monkeys showed signs of depression, as well as inappropriate social behaviors.

René Spitz and Katherine Wolf showed the importance of early attachment for positive psychological development in humans. They observed eighty-eight children under three years of age, who were under the care of eleven attendants. These gloved and psychologically distant caretakers had little time for anything but to take care of the custodial needs of these infants and toddlers. They were unable to hold and hug the children, actions that would have provided much warmth and comfort. By the time Spitz's work was completed, twenty-three of the children were dead, ravaged by relentless medical problems. According to him, the deaths were caused by lack of human attention and affection.

John Bowlby's subsequent work with infants supported this conclusion by demonstrating the need for a secure attachment with at least one parental model early in life. In the early stages of infancy, the infant depends on the parental model, and these needs must be met. With the security provided by attentive parents, the developing child becomes increasingly confident, independent, and psychologically healthy.

Harlow's and Spitz's work shows how the early environment sets the stage for children who fail to thrive, especially under stressful conditions. Thus, according to these attachment theories, the seeds for self-anger, self-disapproval, and even self-destruction are planted early in life.

Cognitive-Behavioral Theories

In recent years, there have been major shifts in theoretical approaches to behavior from a clinical perspective. Cognitive-behavioral psychology has exploded in popularity, and psychologists now concentrate on the importance of guilt, shame, and forgiveness in recovery from dysfunctional states. We believe these emphases can give us new insights into self-destructive processes and allow us to see subtle suicide as something that touches on individual, social, and family dynamics.

Cognitive-behavioral theories do not assume that self-destructive behaviors are unconscious or always rooted in early childhood psychological conflicts. Instead, cognitive-behavioral approaches view self-destruction as based on learning that leads to inappropriate thinking and behavior. According to these theories, self-destructive behavior patterns can be learned at any time, and the learner can be quite conscious of this learning.

Behaviorists see self-destructive acts as maladaptive habits that are shaped and reinforced by their consequences. Studies of operant conditioning show that reinforced behaviors have a higher probability of occurring in the future. Even when we are not aware of this type of connection, we do things repeatedly if we receive something pleasurable as a result. We can assume, therefore, that people who hurt themselves are deriving something positive from this behavior, such as attention or sympathy. Note that the reinforcement does not have to be positive, or even make sense, in the eyes of others. The point is that, for some people, negative attention can be more rewarding than positive attention or no attention at all.

Cognitive theorists say people can develop irrational and illogical thinking that causes them to behave in inappropriate and self-defeating ways. Thus, we can view self-destructive people as those who have learned to think in ways that provide the psychological energy behind subtle suicide. For example, an individual may believe that certain thoughts, feelings, and actions are immoral, and that people who behave in those ways should be severely punished. Consequently, if the individual who holds this belief actually engages in actions he or she feels are immoral (say, masturbation or lying), then the seeds for self-destruction are in place: "I believe certain actions are immoral; I show those actions; therefore, I must punish myself."

Social theorists say we model the behavior of others and are profoundly influenced by the consequences we see others receive for their behavior. In other words, observing someone get rewarded or punished for a certain action can influence the observer's behavior. Thus, if we see others act in self-destructive ways and receive what we see as a reward, such as attention, we might be inclined to act in a similar manner. Children who observe parents acting in careless, neglectful, and self-destructive ways can learn to act the same way in similar circumstances.

Existential Theory

Existential theorists view self-destructive acts, like other patterns of behavior, as a choice. These theorists believe we make our own choices and we alone are responsible for the consequences. This does not mean there are no external factors that cause us to engage in self-destructive behavior. Ultimately, however, we are responsible for our choices, even if our life road has been rocky, such as experiencing a bad childhood or suffering from traumatic environmental events. Existentialists say we choose, or do not choose, to take control of our life in constructive ways. The responsibility is placed directly on our shoulders. Growing up in a disadvantaged home life, for example, is not a legitimate reason to self-destruct in adulthood.

Humanistic Theory

Carl Rogers argued that we are born with an actualizing tendency. In other words, we are genetically programmed with built-in motivation to develop our inherent potentials. It is assumed that, when given the proper environmental ingredients, we will eventually attain our inherent potential. The self-concept is central to this humanistic approach and is seen as a kind of focal point around which personality operates. Put another way, the self is a unifying and stable force within the personality. If not given adequate and appropriate amounts of love and approval, according to Rogers, we will develop a negative self-concept and maladaptive behavior patterns. Low self-esteem can easily lead to a downward spiral that eventually causes self-destruction through behavior patterns like underachievement, poor interpersonal relations, high conformity rates, social anxiety, unhappiness, and drug and alcohol use.

Sociocultural Theory

Émile Durkheim distinguished three types of suicide: egoistic, altruistic, and anomic. *Egoistic suicide* relates to poor integration of the individual into family and social life. *Altruistic suicide* is associated with overintegration of the individual with societal beliefs and customs, sometimes leading to religious or military sacrifice. *Anomic suicide* is correlated with significant changes in economic status, such as experiencing sudden wealth or poverty. Durkheim also included the weakening or breakup of a marriage as a condition facilitating feelings of anomie. Either change can present incredible challenges to the individual.

The concepts of egoistic and anomic suicide appear relevant to the concept of subtle suicide. Durkheim contended that egoistic suicide is more prevalent in cultures that are highly individualistic, and anomic suicide is more prevalent in rapidly changing cultures. Because the United States is rapidly expanding and changing, there is a risk that psychological states associated with heightened self-destructive potential will increase in our society for the foreseeable future.

In his classic work *The Sane Society* (1955), Erich Fromm presented ideas similar to Durkheim's. Fromm said that increasing industrialization produces greater alienation, dissatisfaction, meaninglessness, and apathy in members of a society. He saw the vast majority of people not utilizing their intellectual and creative potentials while having little share in their employer's goals and profits. This state of futility tends to be masked by the individual's compulsive activities or craving for power, money, or prestige. Thus, Fromm saw advanced industrialization as capable of creating, or worsening, psychological distress that can induce suicidal tendencies.

Cost-Reward Theory

A cost-reward analysis integrates biological, cognitive, and behavioral elements. Essentially, this theoretical approach suggests that people want to do things that provide more rewards than costs, and avoid the opposite. The rewards and costs can be both external, such as approval, money, or punishment, and internal, such as self-esteem, guilt, or shame.

With respect to subtle suicide, we believe this model is relevant, because victims are constantly unsure of their commitment to living. They see their lives dominated by costs (negative emotions, physical pain, practical life problems) as opposed to the rewards of living. They get involved in many self-defeating and self-destructive actions that increase costs and reduce pleasure, such as social withdrawal and alienating others. The bottom line is that it is hard to remain committed to a long-term quality life when buried under an avalanche of troubles. Eventually, any built-in desire to live will be replaced by, at best, indifference to life and, at worst, active self-destruction.

Biological Theories

These theories focus on the genetics of self-destructive tendencies. Such theories do not necessarily state a direct relationship between self-destructiveness and genetics, but they do suggest that biological factors can predispose a person to self-destructiveness. In other words, genetic processes can make us vulnerable to dangerous patterns of thinking and behavior that lead to self-destructive tendencies. Some theorists suggest that people can be genetically vulnerable to such disorders as schizophrenia, bipolar, borderline personality, major depression, generalized anxiety, and antisocial personality. These psychological disorders can have profound effects on our functioning and be associated with poor responses to stress and, ultimately, self-destructive tendencies.

Research with twins has found that when one member of an identical pair commits suicide, the other member commits suicide at a rate higher than is true for fraternal twins or siblings. The higher rate, of course, corresponds to a greater genetic similarity in the identical pair than in the fraternal twins or siblings.

What could be the genetic mechanism behind this relationship? Some researchers speculate about serotonin, a brain neurotransmitter. Individuals low in serotonin levels are at a higher risk for suicide and for impulsive aggression. If serotonin levels are influenced by genetic factors, when one member of an identical pair has low levels, the other member will, too, possibly predisposing both to a high suicide risk.

Research has also shown that the spinal fluid of some depressed and suicidal patients has abnormally low amounts of 5-hydroxyindoleacetic acid (5HIAA). This chemical is produced when serotonin is broken down in the body. Once again, genetic mechanisms could be at work in producing these biochemical imbalances, thus serving as a predisposing factor to suicidal ideation and behavior.

We do not, however, want to minimize the potential effects of the environment. It is possible, for instance, that low levels of 5HIAA are also due to high amounts of stress in one's life, which can create various biological changes and negative emotions. Some researchers believe that low 5HIAA levels do not necessarily cause suicide, but make us more vulnerable to suicide by reducing our ability to cope with stressors. Certainly, it is easy to see how both environmental and biological factors can influence and strengthen one another, as well as lead to a variety of negative outcomes, including self-destructive acts.

Acceptance and Commitment Therapy

Acceptance and Commitment Therapy (ACT) is one of the newest and probably the "hottest" orientations in clinical psychology, and we will have a lot more to say about it when we discuss treatment of the subtle suicide victim. So far, analyses of the effectiveness of ACT have been very positive with a variety of disorders (bipolar, borderline, Asperger's, schizophrenia, and drug/alcohol problems).

ACT blends many therapeutic approaches and includes elements from traditional behavioral and cognitive-behavioral orientations, Gestalt, existential, and Eastern methods stressing meditation. ACT therapists do not assume that people who are acting abnormally are abnormal. Rather, they view most people with significant psychological problems as getting into trouble because their mind is behaving the way it was designed through evolution. Thus, the mind operates to insure survival. As a result, we have a strong penchant to avoid unpleasant and painful experiences because they generally are inconsistent with promoting our survival.

According to ACT theory, we are governed by mechanisms to avoid pain and death. Thus, it is easy for our minds to be dominated by defensive actions that may help us survive, even though they may not help us thrive. As a result, we are at risk for developing avoidance behaviors that inevitably lead to lack of spontaneity, underachievement, depression, panic attacks, and other dysfunctions. We try to avoid as much emotional pain as possible, including the normal suffering that is a part of life. Unfortunately, this avoidance allows for short-term relief at the expense of long-term goals and values.

ACT theorists say we cannot escape pain and suffering in life. We can, however, make the commitment to values, goals, and purposes that guide our behavior. Choosing such a path makes it easier to deal with anxiety and other painful experiences. Many people simply exist and live defensively by trying to minimize pain at the expense of their values. They need to look at whether or not their style of life is "working." If not, they need to determine what is getting in their way and stop avoiding these things.

Summary of Theories

Our treatment of theories is neither exhaustive nor comprehensive, and isn't intended to be. We simply want to point out that the concept of subtle suicide is within the scope of previous theorizing about self-destructive behavior tendencies in people. The same conditions these theories say cause other kinds of dysfunctional behaviors can also lead to subtle suicide. All the theories we covered have potential applications to subtle suicide.

HISTORICAL VIEWS OF SUICIDE

We now turn to more specific historical treatments of self-destruction. As we proceed, we will point out similarities and differences between selected earlier treatments of self-destruction and the concept of subtle suicide.

Self-Destructive Behavior

Earlier, we noted the contributions of Karl Menninger to the study of suicidal behavior. Another pioneer was Edwin Schneidman, who developed a classification system based on suicide victims' attitude toward their own death. He proposed that deaths be classified as intentional, subintentional, or unintentional. *Subintentional deaths* refer to ones in which the victim played some hidden or unconscious role in their death. We find examples of such roles in those who follow lifestyles that create or worsen medical problems or who regular perform highly risky behaviors.

In his 1975 work *Self-Destructive Behavior,* Albert Roberts extended the psychodynamic interpretation of self-destructive behavior. He viewed affected individuals as suffering from inability to love and care for themselves. More specifically, he outlined many aspects of self-destructive behavior, including such events as automobile accidents, drug abuse, and chronic depression.

In *The Many Faces of Suicide* (1950), Norman Farberow proposed the concept of indirect self-destructive behavior (ISDB). Like Menninger's approach, which was essentially psychoanalytic, Farberow's work was based primarily on a psychodynamic framework. Prior to Farberow's book, there were numerous works on overt suicide, but almost no discussion of the notion of passive forms of suicide. Farberow's writings, however, focused on what was known at the time about self-injurious and self-destructive behavior, a focus closely related to our concept of subtle suicide. His work expanded knowledge and understanding of ISDB by covering such topics as self-initiated physical illness, drug abuse, obesity, cigarette smoking, self-mutilation, auto accidents, gambling, criminal activity, and other high-risk behaviors. Farberow also outlined the characteristics of ISDB, which yielded a framework from which to conceptualize this type of behavior. The basic characteristics or dimensions of ISDB are listed below, along with our description of subtle suicide victims as we see them within Farberow's framework.

ISDB Characteristics

Physical/Behavioral

- *Farberow analysis:* The person neglects physical appearance and the quality of his or her own behavior. Personal habits are sloppy and careless.
- *Church/Brooks analysis:* Neglectful behavior is common. Physical appearance and personal habits usually deteriorate, but some show no change and others become excessively involved in a meticulous, impeccable appearance.

Cognitive

- *Farberow analysis:* The individual's thought processes are mostly superficial, with little self-insight.
- *Church/Brooks analysis:* Cognitive declines are generally not found, unless there are consequences of drug, alcohol, or medication abuse or some other assault on the brain. Thought processes and insight may or may not be superficial, although insight is more likely to be so. Generally, the person spends a good deal of time and energy trying to ward off painful thoughts and may be aware of an ambivalence about living.

Emotional

- *Farberow analysis:* No significant changes.
- *Church/Brooks analysis:* Changes are expected in sufferers. These changes vary from indifference to marked levels of anxiety, depression, and other negative

emotional states, depending on situational factors and course of condition. Feelings of helplessness and hopelessness are common. Likewise, shame, guilt, and anger are often in the extreme range.

Dynamics

- *Farberow analysis:* The person is oriented toward the present, with little concern for the future or goal achievement. There is poor social adjustment and moderate feelings of inadequacy. Denial tendencies are very strong.
- *Church/Brooks analysis:* Similar to Farberow's, except we note that some victims are fixated on past trauma, experiences, and mistakes. Feelings of inadequacy are often extreme, and denial may or may not be strong.

The Future

- *Farberow analysis:* Victims show little concern for the future; they are unable to delay gratification.
- *Church/Brooks analysis:* Our analysis is similar to Farberow's, with the addition of individual types who are "too good" at delaying gratification and take on a martyr complex. This pattern results in excessive care (to the point of intrusion) given to others, as well as rigid obsessive-compulsive-type actions. Fundamentally, most do not want to live in the future.

Immediate Conditions

- *Farberow analysis:* There is no dominant immediate precipitating stress. Breakdown results from the cumulative impact of preceding events.
- *Church/Brooks analysis:* Subtle suicide results from the cumulative effect of preceding stress, but victims are also under high levels of immediate distress because of their self-defeating behavior patterns and/or life circumstances. This immediate stress is usually superimposed on underlying and preexisting psychological difficulties.

Risk-Taking

- *Farberow analysis:* The person seeks high levels of excitement and risk.
- *Church/Brooks analysis:* Subtle suicide sometimes includes high levels of excitement and risk, but many sufferers show emotional and behavioral constriction while avoiding stimulation and excitement. In fact, this tendency may be so great that it is a fundamental reason for depression and associated difficulties (e.g., social withdrawal) that help make life less worth living.

Coping Mechanisms

- *Farberow analysis:* Typical patterns are denial, avoidance, and suppression of issues and conflicts facing the victim.

- *Church/Brooks analysis:* Subtle suicide involves those mechanisms mentioned by Farberow, but we also see strong signs of displacement of aggressive tendencies away from the source of anger and toward self and others. Many sufferers also attempt to undo guilt by expressing martyrlike patterns, demonstrate obsessive-compulsive tendencies, and/or overuse rationalization and intellectualization as defense mechanisms.

Communication

- *Farberow analysis:* Superficial and devoid of deep meaning. The sufferer implicitly conveys a lack of regard for other people.
- *Church/Brooks analysis:* Although this may be the case, sufferers vary with respect to the depth of their communication, and some show a great deal of empathy toward others. Some demonstrate so much regard for others that they are essentially ignoring their own wants and needs and continue to live for others even though they want to die.

Relationships

- *Farberow analysis:* Victims show minimal investment in relationships. They are self-centered and detached.
- *Church/Brooks analysis:* Once again, some show this pattern, but we also see subtle suicide victims who are excessively overattached and codependent on others.

It is important to note that Farberow's characteristics of ISDB were drawn more from observations of individuals with physical or medical problems, such as diabetics, the chronically ill, and the elderly, than were ours. It is not surprising, therefore, that our ideas differ a bit from Farberow's; we are describing a much broader array of self-destructive individuals, including people with emotionally based coping problems and those with personality disorders. Thus, although we agree with many of Farberow's analyses and observations, we find the need for additions to his analyses to include our broader population of sufferers. We note many differences in the outline above, but we believe some deserve elaboration and are worth reiterating:

- Subtle suicide sufferers may show cognitive declines, especially when self-defeating behaviors such as accidents, alcoholism, or poor self-care are involved.
- Superficial thinking and reasoning are not necessarily present. Some people are quite aware of how their behaviors are self-destructive and what negative ramifications are likely. Some sufferers become very aware of their passive suicide processes.
- Many people we observe with subtle suicide tendencies are in outpatient or inpatient therapy. Quite a few of them, as well as their counterparts who are

not in treatment, have significant emotional difficulties, such as depression, anxiety, guilt, shame, and intense anger. As a matter of fact, most are riddled with intense ambivalence about living. On the one hand, they want desperately to live, but, on the other, they don't care if they live another day.

- Subtle suicide victims often have a long history of life problems and self-destructive behavior patterns. Problems accumulate and can reach a crisis point. But we believe it is essential to investigate thoroughly the current life status of sufferers, because we find many have significant precipitating stressors such as financial and relationship problems, employment loss, death of close loved ones, physical illness or disability, or chronic pain conditions.

- Not all of the people we have observed with subtle suicide seek excessive excitement in their lives. As a matter of fact, many are very much the opposite. That is, they can be very conservative, isolated, compulsive, and/or restrictive individuals. We must not, therefore, rely on risk-taking behavior to identify potential subtle suicide profiles.

- Subtle suicide victims possess varied coping mechanisms. Along with those noted by Farberow, some may overintellectualize through obsessive-compulsive styles, project their problems onto others (e.g., show paranoid patterns), or overuse displacement like the antisocial personality. However, the main coping mechanism is avoidance.

- It is important to realize that ISDB and subtle suicide patterns carry significant and recognizable messages for others. Although the messages conveyed by sufferers tend to be nonverbal and covert, they are nevertheless apparent to others who are sensitive and aware enough to pick them up. Also, some sufferers will be quite open and frank about their state of mind and possess a great deal of empathy for those who choose to "put up with" them.

SUMMARY

Subtle suicide is many things, but it is not masochism. Although Menninger said it is hard to understand why someone would prefer pain to pleasure, he also noted that people often prefer pity to being ignored. He argued that love in the form of pity is preferable to death or desertion.

We also believe that subtle suicide is much more than the ISDB patterns discussed by Farberow. Subtle suicide involves dynamics that extend far beyond those self-destructive behaviors associated with chronic illness, aging, disability, depression, and other similar life experiences.

Like Menninger, Roberts, and Farberow, we hope to build and extend another bridge to the understanding of the importance of the serious form of chronic self-destruction we refer to as subtle suicide. However, theoreticians and researchers have largely ignored covert, passive, subtle forms of self-destruction. There are isolated research studies looking at selective aspects of self-neglect and abuse, but it is hard to find serious comprehensive treatment of this subtle epidemic. We believe that a fresh look at this topic is long overdue. Moreover, recent theoretical and research developments in clinical psychology allow for application of a variety of new and promising approaches to the concept of subtle suicide.

_____ *Chapter 7* _____

Formal Treatment of Subtle Suicide

Treating subtle suicide clients can be tricky, because they show a variety of behavior symptoms that might be seen as the core problem, when the real problem is actually quite different from the symptoms. Unfortunately, when subtle suicide is identified, there is little available information on what special treatment considerations should be taken into account and used. This chapter will focus on what we view as some of the more important aspects to consider when dealing with subtle suicide clients.

In his 1938 work *Man against Himself*, Karl Menninger articulated the basic treatments of self-destructiveness. Menninger's analyses were designed for both passively and actively suicidal individuals. He accepted the Freudian notion of death instinct and saw aggression toward self and others as unavoidable. However, he was optimistic about our ability to handle hostility and internal life-versus-death struggles. Chief among the factors that can aid the life force is love. Menninger wrote: "All psychotherapy depends for its effectiveness on the extent to which the physician is able to give the patient something he needs and cannot get or cannot accept—love" (p. 390). Of course, Menninger used the term *love* in more than a romantic context, covering a broad spectrum of caring, compassion, empathy, and understanding.

Menninger outlined a series of steps in therapy he believed were crucial for reducing self-destructive behavior. He said that treatment begins with building trust and communication with the victim. Once clients allow themselves to become dependent on a "loving" therapist, then their egos can be strengthened and guided by treatment. Generally, treatment involves the following:

1. Increasing insight into the nature of self-destructiveness
2. Understanding motives involved in problematic situations or conflicts, such as the discrepancy between what is desired and the self-destructive behavior

3. Remembering and reworking old conflict and unconscious aggression toward others

4. Developing new friendships and revitalizing current ones such as marriage and parenting relationships

5. Planning for the future in more constructive ways by replacing bad habits with more productive actions. Menninger stressed the importance of creative pursuits and hobbies: "To many people, these seem far more precious than any human friendship could ever be" (p. 385). He believed that involvement in hobbies and creative activities is healthy because they validate the person and allow for expression of unique personality traits.

More recent therapeutic approaches emphasize cognitive-behavioral treatments for such self-destructive acts as self-mutilation, gambling, and alcoholism. There are also many who say support groups like Alcoholics Anonymous or Gamblers Anonymous are good ways to attack what many consider to be addictions or diseases that cause self-destructive behaviors. Finally, numerous professionals believe psychotropic medications are appropriate for treating these problems. Thus, clients who meet our criteria for subtle suicide often receive prescriptions for antidepressants, anti-anxiety agents, and mood stabilizers. Some clients say these medications give them enough relief to make their symptoms more tolerable, which helps them work through their psychological difficulties. Others say they don't feel any different while on medication or discontinue them because of negative side effects.

We see problems with all of these approaches when dealing with the subtle suicide client. The problem is that too often the symptoms tend to be the focus, and it is the symptoms that are treated with medication or psychotherapy. Similarly, supervisors, teachers, parents, friends, and spouses often focus on symptoms when dealing with the subtle suicide victim. For example, parents may complain about their child's low grades, drug or alcohol abuse, or inability to keep a job. Spouses may criticize their partner for lack of sex, low mood, or social withdrawal. Those who make these complaints tend to blame self-defeating behavior on laziness, irresponsibility, immorality, disease, addiction, or hormone problems. Such blame, however, ignores the broad nature of the subtle suicide process and how it can affect many aspects of the sufferer's life. When we focus on symptoms, we also tend to overlook a crucial question: How did the victim get this way? Answering this question is essential to understanding the underlying psychological dynamics of the sufferer, going further than merely saying, for example, "This person has a drinking problem." By focusing on the content of self-defeating or self-destructive acts, we tend to miss the larger pattern of subtle suicide that goes much deeper than the overt symptoms.

It is easy to confuse symptoms with causes. This problem often occurs with depression, which is all too frequently seen as a cause of self-destructive behavior. Certainly, once a person is in the subtle suicide zone, depression can act to maintain negative behaviors. More often, however, we find that people tend to become depressed because of other factors that are actually responsible for the subtle suicide process. These other factors would include such things as psychological, physical, or sexual abuse, emotional deprivation, and chronic avoidance of anxiety and fearful situations. These states typically cause shame, distrust, guilt, low self-esteem, social withdrawal, hostility, and other psychological reactions, which ultimately lead to depression and associated features, including self-destructive acts. Thus, simply targeting depressive symptoms with medication and psychotherapy isn't likely to pay high dividends for the sufferer, because such treatment is not addressing the actual underlying causes of subtle suicide.

We believe the same problems occur with treating so-called addictions. Viewing excessive gambling, drug or alcohol use, sex, Internet use, or eating as "addictions" demonstrates oversimplified and circular reasoning. The reasoning goes something like this: "How do I know Joe has an addiction? Because he drinks uncontrollably. Why does he drink uncontrollably? Because he has an addiction!" What is causing Joe's self-destructive behavior? From this oversimplified perspective, the cause is alcohol addiction, a disease. Thus, the argument goes, we must cure the "disease" if we want to help Joe.

We don't deny that alcoholics have genetic and/or environmental predispositions toward alcohol abuse and dependence. Nevertheless, what we see with subtle suicide victims is that their self-destructive habits result from other factors that precede the alcohol abuse. We saw this process with the case of Ben, who was "different" and developed a gambling problem. We also saw it with Ted, the death challenger, who excessively used alcohol, and with Alice, the drug-abusing attention deficit hyperactivity disorder (ADHD)/learning disability case.

Subtle suicide tendencies develop as a result of a variety of precipitating factors. Then, self-destructive habits like excessive drinking develop and help maintain and worsen the subtle suicide processes. Those around the victim mistakenly believe that the drinking is an addiction and a disease that is the underlying cause of the psychological problems. Thus, we attempt to treat the disease—the drinking, the gambling, the depression, the anxiety—but the treatment doesn't work because we are focusing on the wrong target.

Treatment strategies for subtle suicide must begin from a context of asking, How did this person get derailed from a positive commitment to life? For most of us, a commitment to living takes priority over things like abusing alcohol or drugs, gambling, and other self-defeating actions. When we get pleasure from our work, friendships, love relationships, and hobbies, we are not likely to be ambivalent about living. In fact, we will wake up most days with positive anticipation and a sense of meaning in our life, feeling purposefully directed toward a future. This is not the case, however, with the subtle suicide person.

As our case studies pointed out, things can happen in our lives that sap our will to live and make us vulnerable to self-destructive behavior patterns. Subtle suicide victims learn to direct negative energy, particularly anger, toward themselves. Guilt, shame, and embarrassment often make it difficult for the sufferer to get help. Thus, subtly suicidal people will often not open up enough because they are too ashamed, depressed, or guilty and desperately want to protect their already fragile self-concept.

We believe there are three important components to any treatment strategy for helping subtle suicide victims: early diagnosis, expressing inner feelings, and acceptance of diagnosis.

Early diagnosis. Our case studies show that most subtle suicide processes, like most psychological disorders, begin in childhood and adolescence. People often suffer for many years before receiving professional treatment. This delay in recognition and treatment not only is unfortunate but also can make treatment much more difficult, no matter what the disorder. Delay in treatment means that the victim will probably have developed habitual ways of thinking and acting and that motivation to improve may have decreased significantly. Sufferers see little hope, believing their "die is cast." The wait means that difficult life circumstances are more likely to be present, including unemployment, marital problems, divorce, estrangement from children, and deteriorating physical health. Their self-destructive tendencies have probably lowered the quality of their life to a point where they are no longer committed to positive living. We saw an example of this process vividly in the ADHD/learning disability case, where Alice's careless behaviors led to a positive HIV diagnosis.

Expressing inner feelings. Once subtle suicide tendencies are recognized, the next step is to get victims to open up about their innermost feelings regarding life and living. This can be a tricky step, because people respond differently to this step, and their actions depend on the timing and social skills of the "therapist," whether professional, paraprofessional, friend, spouse, child, or extended family member. We saw many of these principles in the cases of the Army post-traumatic stress disorder victim, the sexually exploited woman with intense shame, and the tragic auto accident victim. It may take a hospitalization and lengthy group therapy experiences to unlock mental doors that have been closed for years or even decades.

On the other hand, in the auto/elevator accident case, we saw an individual who rebounded relatively well with standard outpatient psychotherapy. We suspect many cases that don't come to the attention of psychiatrists and psychologists are handled well by primary care physicians, other medical specialists, friends, teachers, and work supervisors, particularly in the early stages of the process.

We are also aware that "interventions" like those proposed by some support groups (e.g., Alcoholics Anonymous) sometimes work well. In these, a group of concerned family members or significant others confront subtle suicide victims in an effort to get them to see how their behaviors negatively affect themselves as well as others. The intervention strategy can backfire, however, so it needs to be used with caution. Intervention is a powerful emotional tool, but can serve to further alienate subtle suicide sufferers by making them feel more rejected, ashamed, guilty, and worthless. A therapeutic intervention by a professional is generally preferred if the subtle suicide victim will voluntarily engage in such treatment.

Client acceptance of diagnosis. In our case studies, we have seen successes and failures. We have seen victims who needed psychiatric hospitalization, group therapy, and intensive medication before getting better. We have seen others improve with only outpatient psychotherapy. We are quite certain that there are many people who avoid or exit the subtle suicide zone with the help of friends and other nonprofessionals. Whatever the case, however, for those who successfully conquer and exit the subtle suicide zone, we have seen one thing common to success: the importance of personal and "public" awareness and acceptance of the diagnosis.

We have found that when clients are made aware of the dynamics of subtle suicide, and when they are able to identify and accept themselves as fitting the category, they are more likely to be successful in improving their lives. Once they understand and accept their condition, they are able to see how subtle suicide patterns can be therapeutically woven into their life history and current problems. They see new opportunities to reconstruct their lives and change their behaviors, attitudes, and emotions. We also find that at least one other person in the client's life should be made aware of the diagnosis (hence the word "public" in our statement above). This approach tends to increase the sufferer's accountability, give them someone else to open up to, and increase understanding in others who "know."

When presented with the subtle suicide analysis, we find that clients are not only intrigued with the concept but also relieved that someone finally understands their internal conflicts. They feel less alone with their psychological states and experience a sense of comfort that others suffer from similar issues. Exploration of the underlying causes of their subtle suicide process becomes a collaborative part of their therapy. In some cases, their motivation quickly shifts in more positive directions. They stop looking for easy answers (e.g., "Medication will make me better") and realize they have been their own worst enemy. Then, they can finally more clearly see potential choices that would make living more pleasurable. They see the need to put both feet into life and live fully. They come to understand that being ambivalent about living simply does not work because they become more vulnerable to self-destructive behaviors.

These clients discover that previous diagnoses did not help them make sense of their problems. Diagnoses of bipolar disorder, dysthymia, major depression, alcohol dependence, or borderline personality simply did not adequately explain why they were so neglectful, self-mutilating, careless,

or plagued with suicidal thoughts. They saw that others with similar diagnoses did not suffer from these symptoms to the degree they did. The bottom line is that they accepted their lack of commitment to living and how
it affected others, and then made a choice to either continue to live with
their problems or choose more constructive paths.

THE ROLE OF AMBIVALENCE

There is substantial evidence that overtly suicidal patients typically experience ambivalence about ending their lives. Such a feeling is one of the
hallmarks of both overtly and subtly suicidal individuals. As we stated earlier, contemporary research offers some promising new possibilities for
treatment. One of these involves integrative approaches for the treatment
of ambivalence, developed by psychologists David Engle and Harold
Arkowitz. These researchers emphasize that people are often afraid of
change, and their fear makes them resist trying to produce change in their
lives. The resistance causes ambivalence, because one part of them wants
positive change while another part senses the dangers and challenges of
change. The stakes are typically much higher with subtly and overtly suicidal people than with those not struggling with suicide issues. Those issues
deal with the endgame, with the final question, "Do I really want to stop
thinking, feeling, and breathing?"

One of the newer approaches to treating ambivalence is called *motivational interviewing*, developed by clinical psychologists William Miller and
Stephen Rollnick. They list four basic procedures the helper must follow:

1. *Express empathy.* From this perspective, it is crucial that therapists empatheti-
   cally accept that clients' ambivalence about change is normal.
2. *Help to bring out discrepancies between the clients' present behavior and underlying value systems.* Potentially, this effort could help the subtle suicide client
   see that his or her present actions (or lack thereof) are not consistent
   with the values of being an effective parent, good role model, loving spouse,
   and so on.
3. *Explore the pros and cons of change from the perspective of the client.* If therapists do not show understanding and acceptance of clients by pushing too hard
   for constructive change, the clients are more likely to show increased resistance
   to change and are less likely to develop feelings of personal freedom and control. A certain amount of resistance to change is expected, because with positive
   changes comes stress related to fear of failure, increased expectations and
   responsibilities, anxiety related to greater uncertainty, and so forth. The bottom
   line, however, is that clients must choose whether to make their own life
   changes or not.
4. *Increase clients' self-efficacy.* Clients must believe that they can be effective
   agents of change, that they can indeed produce effects in their world through

their actions. As clients increase their feelings of self-efficacy, they will have more confidence in their ability to produce change in their lives, which will make them more likely to undertake such constructive actions.

TREATMENT STRATEGIES

Many treatment strategies are appropriate for subtle suicide individuals. We have no reason to believe that unique treatments need to be applied in such cases. However, it seems clear that many victims have been traumatized as young people. As a result, some may require specialized counseling to help them deal with such underlying emotional issues as anger, shame, and betrayal. Additionally, because their core conflicts typically involve ambivalence about living and frequent suicidal thoughts, some existential techniques may be quite helpful. This type of approach can assist with issues like the meaning of life, death anxiety, fears of abandonment, and existential guilt. It can also be helpful with reducing feelings of aloneness and increasing self-disclosure.

Subtle suicide victims profit greatly from the support and input of others through modified couples/family therapy and support groups. These approaches help the clients feel less alone and remind them there are others who care about their existence. Also, to the extent that others may be enabling the victim's self-defeating and self-destructive symptoms, these orientations can help lessen the rewards received through inappropriate sympathy and attention from others.

MINDFULNESS AND ACCEPTANCE

Some subtle suicide cases are very resistant to treatment because the sufferer has been in the subtle suicide zone for a long time and has spiraled down to extreme depths due to self-defeating behavior patterns. In such cases traditional cognitive-behavioral treatments may not be sufficient. Steven Hayes has been instrumental in developing a promising new approach called acceptance and commitment therapy (ACT), which may add significantly to the therapeutic arsenal in treating the subtle suicidal client by supplementing current approaches.

ACT is part of a "third wave" of therapies that have been developed over the past several decades. During the first wave, behaviorists helped develop therapies grounded on learning principles, which produced such applications as token economies in institutional settings, techniques to facilitate language and attention skills in autistic children, strategies to eliminate phobias and speech anxiety problems, and programs to help people stop drinking or overeating. The second wave of cognitive therapies gave professionals techniques to treat a wider array of psychological problems by attacking irrational thinking patterns. Unfortunately, these methods are not effective with some clients; attempts to get patients to replace irrational or distorted thoughts with more reasonable ones, or engage in "thought stopping," are not always possible or even sufficient. ACT represents the third wave of therapies to aid in combating distress in people who have been unable to help themselves or have not received sufficient treatment via more traditional psychotherapeutic means.

The ACT approach suggests that we let go of trying to control unwanted and unpleasant thoughts and feelings. Not only is suppression of thoughts and feelings generally ineffective, but it also reduces awareness of how our feelings and thoughts are connected to how we behave. "Letting go" means no longer trying to control unpleasant thoughts and feelings. The process can help us accept the presence of negative feelings and thoughts and understand that they are simply a natural part of being human.

ACT also says we need to accept the fact that our thoughts and feelings are not necessarily based on reality; they are just thoughts and feelings. We don't have to control them, be influenced by them, or get overly attached to them. In effect, we can let them go in one side of our brain and out the other. In "Mindfulness-Based Cognitive Therapy" (2004), ACT theorists Zindel Segal, John Teasdale, and Mark Williams assert: "Instead of viewing thoughts as absolutely true or as descriptive of important self-attributes, patients are able to see negative thoughts and feelings as passing events in the mind that are not necessarily valid reflections of reality or central aspects of the self" (p. 9). Thus, by being more objective about our feelings and thoughts, we are more likely to confront situations that frighten or depress us.

The concept of ACT emphasizes how to make more productive choices in life that are consistent with a client's values. There are numerous techniques available that can help motivate our clients to be persistent in getting rid of actions that compromise personal values. For example, suppose we have a client who was sexually abused as a child. Suppose further that this client values intimacy with a lover. Because of the history of abuse, however, the client has strong thoughts and emotions that produce avoidance responses which keep the client distant from the lover both physically and emotionally. Notice that the thoughts and emotions literally force the client into undesirable actions. These actions seem necessary to the client because of anxiety and fear of intimacy based on early abuse. Burdened with these undesirable thoughts and feelings, the client is likely to try to suppress or at least minimize these thoughts and feelings. Unfortunately, this attempt only serves as a form of denial and prevents the client from seeing how the thoughts and feelings are controlling his or her life in negative ways. According to ACT, therefore, the client must stop trying to suppress the negative thoughts and emotions, learn to stop avoiding them, come to accept them, and ultimately begin to see them as unrealistic emotions and thoughts that are keeping the client and lover emotionally and physically distant.

ACT uses exercises designed to increase values clarification and persistence in facing undesirable thoughts and emotions. Exercises are also designed to expose clients to situations they are trying to avoid and help them become more aware of objective reality. The process can be complicated if a client does not have a well-developed value system to work with. Most, however, can be helped to build new behaviors, activities, relationships, purposes, and goals that can ultimately transform into new values.

Strict cognitive-behavioral approaches have been very effective with a wide variety of psychological problems, most notably ones within specific areas, such as speech anxiety, phobias, and controlling personal habits. ACT is a broader orientation that has the potential to reach the core of deeper, lengthier dysfunctional processes such as subtle suicide. ACT includes approaches derived from behaviorism, Eastern philosophy, existential/Gestalt therapies, and social psychology. Its approaches are based on the belief that we are all vulnerable to becoming our own worst enemy. We punish ourselves with critical self-evaluations, and we flood ourselves with negative thoughts that increase anxiety, depression, and self-defeating actions.

ACT theory says we must recognize that human suffering is inevitable. When we don't accept this basic fact, there is an increased risk of dysfunctional consequences. Of course, we all want to avoid fires, car accidents, and life-threatening diseases. However, millions of people won't get on an airplane, avoid going out in public, and will not socialize without alcohol or a prescription medication. According to the ACT model, these types of avoidance actions are caused, at least to some extent, by an inability to handle negative thoughts and to follow a committed path consistent with one's value systems.

Our national health system and the media tell us we need to be continuously strong, happy, rich, and vivacious. Health reports on the nightly news, along with popular shows and advertisements on television and in magazines, constantly show us that we are not living up to ideal standards. As a result, many of us begin to ask, "What is wrong we me? Why am I not as happy as I should be—more successful, more attractive …?" It is not difficult to understand how the next step develops, as one starts seeing the problem as, "I am a [depressed/unhappy/anxious] person."

How do we get to this point? We need to realize that in seeking causes of our problems, we are often mistaken about them and tend to overlook or ignore the real reasons for our emotional states. Many behavior theorists and researchers, in fact, believe we have not evolved to a point where we can accurately understand why we act the way we do. Moreover, we must resist explaining the reasons for our problems by appealing to the emotions themselves. That is, we should not conclude that our thoughts are the reasons for our dilemmas. Some clients say, "The reason I am functioning the way I am is because I am depressed" (or anxious, addicted, or whatever the case may be). Clients believe their thoughts and feelings are the causes of their dysfunctions. Thus, states like depression and anxiety are viewed not only as the *problem* but also the *cause* of the difficulties. Clients come to view their negative emotional states as the reason they can't love, work, or play effectively. The truth of the matter, however, is that they are depressed because of their social withdrawal, their avoidance of responsibility or conflict, an unsatisfying relationship, or something along those lines.

If we believe our emotions and thoughts are the cause of our problems, we will attempt to manage, control, and even avoid those thoughts and emotions. We will feel compelled to control our depressive and anxious feelings and thoughts. But this approach will not work. When we attempt to control our negative thoughts and feelings, they actually become more frequent and troublesome; thought suppression rarely works, and it usually results in frustration, agitation, and demeaning self-talk.

ACT therapists help clients be more accepting of their thoughts and feelings in the sense that they are just that—mere thoughts and feelings. We don't have to be so negatively affected and bothered by our thoughts and feelings. When we are so bothered, ACT therapists say we become fused to our feelings, as though our thoughts and feelings become who we are. We should not avoid them in our present, but should simply tell ourselves they are nothing but thoughts and feelings, and accept them as just that. This recognition will help us be less self-critical and upset with our lives, especially when we don't match up with our own and society's ideals. A certain amount of suffering in life is natural and expected. We are not weird or abnormal just because we experience troubling thoughts or feelings.

According to the ACT model, we need to learn to walk through our suffering while continuing to live a life committed to our values. In other words, it is vital to accept our pain without giving into tendencies to engage in some form of escape or avoidance and run from stress. Drug or alcohol abuse, social withdrawal, gambling, eating disorders, and other acts of escape and avoidance are likely to magnify and expand our problems while taking us further away from our value systems. If we value our roles as parent, spouse, employee, friend, or lover but at the same time let ourselves become less effective in these roles, how can we expect to feel better about ourselves?

From these perspectives, subtle suicide victims may benefit from a more objective, realistic view of their thoughts and feelings. Moreover, they could be helped to live more in the present and be less influenced by their painful and unpleasant history. Furthermore, the victims must realize that their negative thoughts and feelings are not who they are nor necessarily the causes of their problems. The ACT approach, therefore, places the responsibility on sufferers to decide what they truly want. If they value work, family, and friends, it is up to them to act accordingly and to do so with a sincere commitment and dedication. On the other hand, if they don't value life, then it is within their right and discretion to self-defeat and self-destruct.

ACT therapists use a variety of techniques to produce the types of changes we have discussed. For instance, many clients worry too much about, "How well am I doing?" or, "Am I happy enough?" As a result, they lose their ability to feel satisfied in the present. For example, chronically depressed and anxious people are likely to focus on whether or not they are feeling better. As they search for cues in social situations, they may check to see how they are doing. "Does Joe see I'm here?" "Do I look foolish to Sally?" They also monitor their own actions: "Is my heart racing?" "Am I sweating?" "Am I just pretending?" "How well am I relating?" They try to feel "right," which makes it impossible to be themselves and have a good time.

We see similar inappropriate actions in obsessive-compulsive individuals, who attempt to monitor and avoid thoughts or feelings of doom. We see these actions in panic-disordered people who try to avoid losing control or going crazy. These natural but inappropriate reactions to fears and anxieties cause these people to constantly monitor what's going on around them; they continually check on their own actions and worry about what others are thinking; they attempt to maintain complete control of what's going on around them all the time, an impossible task. Thus, these actions are not a solution, but are in fact the problem. In the final analysis, it is fear and anxiety that are the underlying issues most people have to face; fear and anxiety are the bases for the conflicts that produce most of our psychological problems. These conflicts are much more intense in the case of subtle suicide victims, and their challenge is to get more into living and less into avoiding—to live, not simply exist, while facing their fears.

We believe that specialized treatment of severe self-destructive patterns such as subtle suicide is in the infancy stage. We have no doubt that conventional therapies have been used successfully, but we see evidence that many subtle suicide victims are not benefiting from conventional outpatient or inpatient therapies. Many of these people are only receiving medications on an outpatient basis or are receiving cursory therapies in an inpatient setting. Worse yet, many are not being treated at all. Research has shown that about 30 percent of our population meets the criteria for at least one psychiatric disorder during the previous year and approximately 50 percent during their lifetime. Obviously, nowhere near these percentages actually receive any form of formal treatment. We would expect that subtle suicide sufferers are overrepresented among those who are not in treatment, because they are in a state of mind in which they typically don't care what happens to them and tend to terminate treatment prematurely.

In consideration of these realities, it seems logical to conclude that public awareness education should be particularly helpful with getting some subtle suicide victims engaged in self-help or some type of psychiatric/ psychological treatment. As we have seen, a variety of therapies may be applied, including more contemporary styles like ACT. It will be interesting to see what types of approaches work best with this difficult-to-reach client.

_____ *Chapter 8* _____

Measuring Subtle Suicide

IS SUBTLE SUICIDE REAL?

How do we know the concept of subtle suicide actually exists? Frankly, we don't—but then almost all concepts in psychology are neither tangible nor proven. We infer learning, memory, personality, motivation, intelligence, creativity, development, and other significant concepts from observations of behavior.

A more representative and specific example for our purposes is the concept of *learned helplessness* developed by Martin Seligman. No one has ever directly observed this construct, but it has been inferred from observations of behaviors and experiments with animals. We feel learned helplessness is a subset of the larger but related issue of subtle suicide. That is, subtle suicide sufferers often show a pattern of having learned to think and act in helpless ways, causing them to stop trying to avoid negative circumstances. However, we believe subtle suicide victims have a constellation of many other symptoms that plague them, distinguishing them from someone who is merely suffering from learned helplessness. A crime victim may be hesitant to testify against perpetrators, saying, "What's the point? Their lawyer will get them off and then they'll come after me!" This response represents learned helplessness, but is a far cry from the symptoms and dynamics of the subtle suicide victims we have seen throughout this book.

We certainly cannot ethically perform experimental studies to try to create learned helplessness or subtle suicide in people. We do, however, have animal studies demonstrating the dynamics of learned helplessness. Of course, arguments can be made that neither human studies on learned helplessness nor subtle suicide could ever correspond exactly with animal behavior in experiments. Results from animal studies do not definitively explain why adults quit looking for a job, stop trying to resolve marital problems, or refuse to fight a physical illness. Likewise, depriving infant monkeys of social interaction and mother love, and then observing depression and self-destructive behaviors in them, does not directly correspond with subtle suicide. However, parallels exist, and combined with extensive observations from clinical practice, we see a compelling argument for subtle suicide as a valid concept. Thus, we believe efforts to confirm the process should continue with both clinical and naturalistic observations and through the development of a formal assessment instrument.

NEED FOR AN ASSESSMENT INSTRUMENT

As we saw earlier, our notion of subtle suicide is not on one-to-one correspondence with Norman Farberow's notion of indirect self-destructive behavior. However, they overlap a good deal. Our criteria for subtle suicide are similar to Farberow's, although we envision our concept as broader. Research needs to verify and refine subtle suicide criteria by finding out which tend to be mostly closely associated with subtle suicide. Obviously this is a crucial step in validating subtle suicide beyond a case study type of analysis, as these criteria could be used to distinguish subtle suicide victims from those without this condition.

We think, for instance, that some people suffering from anorexia, major depression, bipolar disorder, borderline personality, alcoholism, and anti-social personality are subtly suicidal, but others are not. We believe this distinction is crucial to treating the "whole person," which includes the silent killer, subtle suicide. We are confident that victims who have a subtle suicide diagnosis in addition to conditions like those above, because of their tendency toward noncompliance, will be more resistant to psychotherapy and respond less favorably to psychotropic medications than those without the added diagnosis of subtle suicide. Similarly, we believe they will suffer more frequently from suicidal ideation and attempts and be psychiatrically hospitalized more often than those who are not subtle suicide sufferers but have the same additional diagnoses. We also believe subtle suicide victims will show more failed attempts at rehabilitation, reduced life expectancy, and poorer health status. In order to demonstrate these differences, it is necessary to develop an instrument that can objectify the presence of the condition and to identify degrees of subtle suicide tendencies. We believe such a questionnaire can be developed from the criteria presented in this book.

The major advantages of a reliable and valid questionnaire to measure subtle suicide would be earlier diagnosis and treatment. Most subtle suicide conditions appear to begin in childhood and adolescence, and it seems clear that this is an optimal time for assessment. It would be interesting to investigate whether subtle suicide criteria are the same for children, adolescents, and adults. Certainly it is possible that somewhat different criteria apply across the life span, in which case different questionnaires may need to be constructed.

Thomas Nelson and Norman Farberow developed a fifty-six-item questionnaire designed to "indicate life-threatening behavior." The scales were noted by nursing staff over seven days. Subsequently, Pamela Reed modified their scale to a seventeen-item one that measures degree of harmfulness of behaviors related to maintaining health or predicting future medical problems. The measures were based upon repeated observations made by health-care professionals. We are, however, not aware of any assessment device that objectively yields reliable and valid data on subtle suicide types from self-reports. We believe this kind of instrument would be an important step forward and would help us evaluate whether interventions are having positive effects. Not all subtly suicidal victims could be expected to offer valid self-reports, of course, especially in the early stages of their suffering.

Many researchers have noted that some individuals demonstrate potentially self-destructive behavior patterns but are neither passively nor blatantly suicidal. Examples of such cases include elderly people who show cries for help as they struggle with chronic and debilitating medical conditions. Others include the behaviors of prostitutes, skydivers, alcoholics, accident-prone drivers, and self-mutilaters. As a result, some have argued for the importance of looking at the underlying motivation for self-destructive acts.

Jane Thibault distinguishes between three different underlying causes or motives for indirect life-taking threatening behavior (ILTB): passive suicide, noncompliance, and personal control. Passive suicide is the type most closely related to our concept of subtle suicide. However, ILTB may be caused by cognitive impairment, memory loss, paranoia, and other factors that contribute to noncompliance. Alternatively, elderly adults may feel they have little choice but to gain attention from doctors, nurses, or family members by jeopardizing their health through self-injury. Actually, these actions may be adaptive responses in an attempt to gain control over what they perceive to be negative life situations. In this case, ILTB may prolong their survival. In this type of situation, it is vital that clients be heard and given as much appropriate control over their life situation as possible, in order that they have optimal self-esteem and fewer feelings of helplessness.

We believe comprehensive assessment should involve psychological testing, including a subtle suicide survey when possible. There should also be a clinical overview of the sufferer that uses interviews; a review of psychosocial history; input from doctors, nurses, teachers, and other professionals; and collateral input from significant others. This broad input would lead to a higher proportion of correct diagnoses with respect to three levels of self-destruction proposed below. Without such comprehensive assessment, many subtle suicide victims will go unnoticed, and their underlying conflicts and issues will be neither addressed nor understood.

```
←-------------------------------------------------------------------------------------→
        Self-damaging Behavior          Subtle Suicide          Overt Suicide
```

Figure 8.1
Continuum of Self-Destruction

We see self-destruction on a continuum of severity from self-damaging acts (low end) to overt suicide (high end), as depicted in figure 8.1. We feel that adult humans not only experience different degrees of self-damaging and self-defeating thoughts and behaviors but can also slide down the continuum of self-destruction to dangerous levels. What may have begun as simple acts of self-neglect or abuse to get attention, or short-term relief from distressing thoughts and situations, can materialize into a more serious process of self-destruction. Once indirect or direct forms of self-damage become habitual, they may both preclude more adaptive and constructive behavior patterns and, at the same time, further alienate the sufferer from self and others.

Other psychological and physical problems may mount, while the sufferer's ability to tolerate self-abuse and self-neglect are likely to increase. Along the way, social withdrawal and shame may increase, and social support is likely to dwindle. At this point, we have a sufferer who feels even more alone with personal problems at a time when the need to feel connected and supported is especially intense. All of these forces can create more pressure for relief from self-destruction and even self-punitive actions. It is clear we must enter into the helping process with these sufferers as soon as possible with the most effective interventions.

It is important to distinguish the level of self-destruction that is present. Certainly, we do not want to reinforce self-damaging (but not suicidal) acts with attention and sympathy. On the other hand, we don't want to assume that the subtly or overtly suicidal person is simply seeking attention. Our intervention efforts will differ depending upon where we perceive the sufferer falls on the self-destructive continuum. Along these lines, we have found that educating subtle suicide clients about this process has helped keep some from moving farther along the path of self-destruction and even stopped their self-destructive acts. Others, of course, will require intense treatment efforts to reduce or eliminate self-destructive tendencies, while some will not respond to any formal or informal treatment efforts.

DEVELOPMENTAL FACTORS

Recently, we asked a class of undergraduate psychology college students to develop a summary of someone they knew, past or present, who met the criteria for subtle suicide. Many wrote about a friend who was probably on the road to becoming a victim but was not quite there yet. That is, the students noted the beginnings of self-destructive and self-defeating behaviors that seemed to put their subject on a slow downward spiraling road. The assignment made it clear to students that there are developmental aspects to subtle suicide. This is a common theme in our case studies: most of the victims showed seeds of conflict and the beginnings of subtle suicide in childhood or adolescence. As they grew into middle age and beyond, their condition gained momentum and worsened. Thus, the earlier we can assess and diagnose subtle suicide, the more likely we will be to prevent the worsening downward spiral that tends to occur as the victim ages.

These observations also raise the issue of possible parallels between subtle and overt suicide. For instance, will early detection of subtle suicide help in reducing suicide rates? As Marv Miller pointed out in his book *Suicide after Sixty* (1979, p. 23), "Suicidal episodes among young people are often characterized by gestures which typically do not cause death." On the other hand, geriatric suicide attempts are usually serious. Miller explains, "Many older suicidal people do not want to be rescued because they have conditions which cannot be significantly improved" (p. 23). Thus, elderly individuals are more likely to experience feelings of helplessness and to see life as hopeless. Young people deal better with relationship breakups, job losses, and family problems and are often less demoralized than older people who face cancer, diabetes, widowhood, and impending death. They see they have more time and opportunity to improve their lives. Nevertheless, both young and old need to find hope, or else they will be vulnerable to both subtle and overt suicide. According to Miller, "Lying dormant in all of us is an extremely personal equation which determines the point where the quality of our lives would be so pathetically poor we would no longer wish to live" (p. 8).

A review of our case studies suggests that subtle suicide usually advances like a slow-acting virus. Some of these developmental dynamics involve the following:

- Self-defeating and self-destructive behaviors cause a predictable spiraling down effect.

- Youthful optimism and naïveté eventually give way to pessimism and hopelessness.

- In midlife and beyond, we become increasingly introspective and look back more. Thus, we may punish ourselves with regrets and feel it's too late to change.

- As we get older, we lose reserve capacity. That is, we have less physical capacity to combat stress and attempt to turn our lives around.

- When younger, we have built-in purposes and structures (e.g., school, establishing independence, taking care of children, etc.). As we age, we need to find new purposes and meanings—a difficult process when the nest is empty, our parents are gone, and our career has become a job.

- Young people feel they have time to make changes and "right the ship." As we age, however, our windows of opportunity seem to close one by one.

Because some subtle suicide victims eventually do commit suicide, assessment and treatment may help us understand the overt suicide process better and improve prevention. Additionally, detection of subtle suicide could help streamline psychotherapy with more timely and effective treatment.

The possibility of saving lives and improving the quality of life for victims is extremely encouraging. Still, we feel the need to temper our optimism with some sobering realism. Not all subtle suicide victims will be open to change or professional intervention. Also, by the time some people receive help, they will be beyond repair. Some will simply not have the personal resources or motivation to make constructive change in their lives. For many sufferers, the no-treatment option will apply. That is, for some we will simply be wasting our time, energy, and money in trying to treat them. We believe, however, that the no-treatment option would occur much less frequently if we identified and treated individuals earlier.

CONTEMPORARY INDUSTRIALIZED SOCIETY

The main purpose of this book was to revive and update the idea in psychology that we can turn against ourselves and be our own worst enemy. We believe that subtle suicide is a concept that should be investigated through systematic research. Although case studies are an important way to gather data and generate relevant hypotheses and theories, understanding subtle suicide will require solid research and measurement if the concept is to be useful. Fortunately, there are many theories and research methods available to analyze subtle suicide.

We believe that understanding subtle suicide behavior has never been more important. In modern society, it is becoming easier to self-destruct quickly and effortlessly with convenient access to drugs, weapons, and other dangerous items. Also, we seem to be growing more alienated from others due to technological advances. As practical as they are, such things as email, automated customer service, working at home, and distance learning are taking us farther and farther from direct and intimate contact with real people. At the same time, life in our society is becoming more stressful. The treadmill of change keeps going faster and faster, and the media keep us aware of all kinds of real and potential traumas like terrorist attacks.

We are also becoming increasingly detached from the feeling of productivity and creativity, and less meaningfully engaged in our work. Corporate takeovers, downsizing, increased automation, outsourcing, and company greed have greatly threatened integrity, a healthy work ethic, motivation, independence, and the security of millions of workers. Hardly a day goes by without hearing some corporate horror story, and even successful organizations often squeeze their employees to work harder for less. Too often, it appears that what we've done in the past is irrelevant; what you are doing for me today is all that matters.

We live in a society where many believe style and status are more important than substance. Magazines like *People* repeatedly show the same "beautiful" individuals week after week, and images that perpetuate the idea that "you are what you own and who you know." The message focuses on the artificiality of people's lives, stressing the importance of what you wear, with whom you were seen, where you live, and how much money you make. It is difficult for many Americans to feel a strong sense of self-esteem if they feel they fall short of the ideals that bombard them on a daily basis.

We also live in a society where certain behaviors and feelings, particularly negative ones, are supposed to be suppressed. Children in many schools are not permitted to play outside because they might get hurt and the school might get sued. Sexual harassment, Protection from Abuse court orders, drunk driving, and other legal entanglements are getting more and more frequent. Anger management classes have multiplied, and courts force many people into them. Get yourself into a tirade at work or home and see what happens! We are no longer permitted to lose our temper, no matter how frustrating our life becomes. It's no surprise that right behind anger management programs, assertiveness training programs have been so popular the past twenty to thirty years. We are afraid to speak, much less act, out of fear that we will be sued or lose our jobs.

SUMMARY

We believe subtle suicide is quite prevalent in American society. Cross-culturally, we can only wonder about the frequency of subtle suicide in less industrialized, third world countries. We can only speculate about questions such as whether suicide terrorists are more likely to have been subtly suicidal than nonterrorists. Within our own society, we can ask ourselves whether members of cults and gangs are more likely to be subtly suicidal than nonmembers. These are only a few of many questions about subtle suicide prevalence that have crossed our minds to date.

On a more individual level, the developmental aspects of subtle suicide are varied and fascinating. Most of our case study sufferers were well on their way to subtle suicide before they even had the ability to fend off this process. At the same time, it appears that in many cases, entering the subtle suicide zone was mostly either unconscious or only partially conscious. Moreover, many of those we analyzed seemed to have had a subtle suicide process that was dormant for years or even decades before it flourished, like a cancer suddenly moving into advanced stages.

Usually, advancement of the subtle suicide process into a more extreme form or crisis stage is seemingly stimulated by external pressures (e.g., relationship loss or breakup, threatened or real job loss, deterioration in physical functioning, traumatic experience). Whereas many people would respond to these types of stressors in constructive ways, the subtle suicide victim appears to be predisposed to destructive styles of coping. Shame, low self-esteem, and a penchant for turning anger inward are just some of the common factors that lead subtle suicide sufferers to be self-defeating or to show aggression toward themselves, thus making their life situation worse and diminishing further their will to live.

We also found evidence in our cases that the subtle suicide process often gets stronger in middle age and beyond. At the same time, there are probably many people who defeat the subtle suicide process at a relatively young age before it becomes fully manifest. Experiences with family, friends, coworkers, and outpatients are consistent with this conclusion. Still, it would be interesting to investigate the factors that help protect people from subtle suicide tendencies—things like positive social support systems, high degrees of self-efficacy, a sense of purpose and meaning in life, the capacity to be intimately connected with others, hopeful orientations toward living, a generally positive self-concept, and freedom from intense physical pain and psychological trauma.

We continue to ask if people who become subtle suicide victims as the result of primarily physical discomforts and disabilities may differ from those whose processes are fundamentally psychological in nature. It seems that the former are more likely to be consciously aware of the onset and causes of their condition, which often appear quickly. Also, it seems probable that medical sufferers see themselves as less responsible for their condition. Of course, people who already handle stress poorly are probably more likely to become subtle suicide victims when they experience serious medical problems and physical discomforts. Therefore, we need to ask what differences in treatment strategies might be appropriate for medical versus psychological risk factors. We are not aware of any research that addresses this issue.

In closing, we hope that this book has helped to introduce what we believe will someday become an accepted psychological construct. We would like to see it stimulate discussions, theories, and research on subtle suicide. We do not want our work to stop at a case study analysis and hope that the theories are translated into applications that can help people deal with this real problem. All of us are given a finite amount of time on earth. If we waste our time, we are wasting our life. Subtle suicide individuals waste much of their life. If our work can help somehow in minimizing this process, then we have met our goal. We strongly believe this will be the case. We have seen both clients and families find comfort and direction from learning about the concept of subtle suicide. Moreover, we have seen victims themselves become recommitted to living when they recognize themselves as fitting the subtle suicide syndrome. We have found it immensely rewarding to see some of these sufferers rise from the living dead and lift great burdens both from themselves and their families and friends.

Appendix: Subtle Suicide Questionnaire

Assign to each of the ten items below a number corresponding to the following scale:

Agree Strongly	1
Agree Moderately	2
Agree Slightly	3
Neutral/Uncertain	4
Disagree Mildly	5
Disagree Moderately	6
Disagree Strongly	7

_____   1.   I have felt hopeless about my future for some time now.

_____   2.   For some time now, there has been a part of me that wants to live and go on with my life and another that doesn't care whether I die.

_____   3.   I have struggled with a desire to hurt myself directly or indirectly for a year or more.

_____   4.   Others have said to me that I seem to want to hurt myself.

_____   5.   I have felt helpless to change significant aspects of my life for more than the past year.

_____   6.   Frequently, I give up on trying to cope with or change my life because living hasn't been important to me for some time.

_____   7.   I have struggled with suicidal ideation for an extended period now.

_____   8.   If it were not for my relationship with certain people, I would have committed suicide.

_____   9.   Characteristically, I frequently experience intense negative emotional states such as shame, guilt, anger, or depression.

_____ 10.   If I died in an accident, that would be okay.

Our preliminary analyses suggest that a score of 15 or less is at least moderately predictive of a subtle suicide condition. A score of 16–25 suggests the possibility of subtle suicide or the development of it in the future. Remember, however, this is an informal instrument and should not be taken as a formal diagnosis of a psychological condition.

Bibliography

PART I

Discussions of suicide, both overt and indirect, and some recent demographic statistics on suicide in America can be found in the following:

Bongar, B. (1991). *The suicidal patient: clinical and legal standards of care*. Washington, D.C.: American Psychological Association.

Kessler, R. C., et al. (2005). Trends in suicide ideation, plans, gestures and attempts in the United States. *Journal of the American Medical Association, 293*(20), 2487–2495.

Mann, J. J., Brent, D. A., & Arango, V. (2001). The neurobiology and genetics of suicide and attempted suicide: A focus on the serotomergic system. *Neuropsychopharmacology, 24*(5), 467–477.

Meerlo, J. A. M. (1994). Hidden suicide. In H. L. P. Resnik (Ed.), *Suicidal behaviors: Diagnosis and management* (pp. 82–89). Boston: Little, Brown.

Miller, M. (1979). *Suicide after sixty*. New York: Springer.

National Youth Violence Prevention Resource Center. (2003). Youth suicide facts. Retrieved August 2, 2005, from http://www.feyouth.org/scripts/faq/suicide facts.asp.

Reed, P. G. (1988). Epidemiology and measurement of indirect self-destructive behavior in chronically ill elderly. Unpublished research report, University of Arizona.

Selzer, M. L., & Payne, C. E. (1962, September). Automobile accidents, suicide and unconscious motivation. *Psychiatric Evaluation, 237*–240.

Selzer, M. L., Rogers, J. E., & Kern, S. (1968). Fatal accidents: The role of psychopathology, social stress, and acute disturbance. *American Journal of Psychiatry, 124*, 1028–1036.

Thibault, J. M., O'Brien, J. G., & Turner, C. L. (1999). Indirect life-threatening behavior in elderly patients, *Journal of Elder Abuse and Neglect, 11*, 21–32.

We based our discussion of Evel Knievel, Marilyn Monroe, Jim Morrison, and Anna Nicole Smith on biographical material from the following:

Barris, G. (1995). *Marilyn: Her life in her own words*. New York: Kensington.
Mandich, S. (2000). *Evel incarnate: The life and legend of Evel Knievel*. London: Sedwich & Jackson.
Redding, E., & Redding, D. (2007). *Great big beautiful doll*. Fort Lee, N.J.: Barricade Books.
Saraceno, J. (2007, January 3). Long-retired daredevil frail, feisty, still cheating death. *USA Today,* pp. A1–A2.
Sereg, V. (2008). *Jim Morrison: The poet and the singer*. New York: Verlag.
Spoto, D. (1993). *Marilyn Monroe: The biography*. New York: Kensington.

PART II

We based our coverage on the classic theoretical positions of suicide on the following:

Blum, D. (2002). *Love at Goon Park: Harry Harlow and the science of affection*. Cambridge, Mass.: Perseus.
Durkheim, E. (1951). *Suicide: A study in sociology*. New York: The Free Press.
Ellis, A. (1962). *Reason and emotion in psychotherapy*. New York: Stuart.
Engle, D. E. & Arkowitz, H. (2006). *Ambivalence in Psychotherapy*. New York: The Guilford Press.
Fromm, E. (1941). *Escape from freedom*. New York: Farrar & Rinehart, Inc.
Fromm, E. (1955). *The sane society*. New York: Holt.
Harlow, H. F. (1962). Development of affection in primates. In E. L. Bliss (Ed.), *Roots of behavior*. New York: Harper.
Harlow, H. F. (1964). Early social deprivation and later behavior in the monkey. In A. Abrams, H. H. Gurner, & J. E. P. Tomal (Eds.), *Unfinished tasks in the behavioral sciences*. Baltimore: Williams & Wilkins.
May, R., Angel, E., & Ellenberger, H. F. (Eds.). (1958). *Existence: A new dimension in psychiatry and psychology*. New York: Basic Books.
McCullough, M. E., Pargament, K. I., & Thoresen, C. E. (2000). *Forgiveness: Theory, research and practice*. New York: The Guilford Press.
Menninger, K. (1938). *Man against himself*. New York: Harcourt, Brace.
Miller, W. R., & Rollnick, S. (2002). *Motivational interviewing: Preparing people for change* (2nd ed.). New York: The Guilford Press.
Roberts, A. R. (1975). *Self-destructive behavior*. Springfield, Ill.: Charles Thomas.
Rogers, C. (1951). *Client-centered therapy: Its current practice implications and therapy*. Boston: Houghton Mifflin.
Seligman, M. E. P. (1975). *Helplessness*. San Francisco: Freeman.
Spitz, R. A., & Wolf, K. M. (1946). Anaclitic depression: An inquiry into the genesis of psychiatric conditions in early childhood. *Psychoanalytic Study of the Child, 2,* 313–342.
Tangney, J. D., & Dearing, R. L. (2004). *Shame and guilt*. New York: The Guilford Press.

Farberow's theory is developed in the following sources:

Farberow, N. L. (1980). *The many faces of suicide*. New York: McGraw-Hill.
Nelson, F. L., & Farberow, N. L. (1977). Indirect suicide in the elderly, chronically ill patient. *Suicide Research*, 125–139.
Schneidman, E. S. (1970). Orientations toward death. In E. S. Schneidman, N. L. Farberow, & R. E. Litman (Eds.), *The psychology of suicide* (pp. 3–45). New York: Jason Aronson.

Acceptance and commitment therapy is summarized in the following sources:

Hayes, S. C., Follette, V. M., & Linehan, M. M. (2004). *Mindfulness and acceptance: Expanding the cognitive-behavioral tradition*. New York: Guilford Press.
Hayes, S. C., Strosahl, K. D., & Wilson, K. G. (2003). *Acceptance and commitment therapy: An experimental approach to behavior change*. New York: Guilford Press.
Segal, Z. V., Teasdale, J. D., & Williams, M. E. (2004). Mindfulness-based cognitive therapy: Theoretical rationale and empirical status. In S. C. Hayes, V. M. Follette, & M. M. Linehan (Eds.), *Mindfulness and acceptance: Expanding the cognitive-behavioral tradition* (pp. 45–65). New York: Guilford Press.

Index

About the Authors

MICHAEL A. CHURCH is Associate Professor of Psychology at King's College in Wilkes-Barre, Pennsylvania. He received his bachelor's degree in psychology from California State University at Fullerton, and his master's and doctoral degrees in psychology from the University of Miami. He has taught at King's College since 1976, and has been a licensed clinical psychologist with a private practice since 1980. He performs psychological testing and group therapy at First Hospital Wyoming Valley, Kingston, PA. He is a member of the Council of National Register of Health Service Providers in Psychology. He is co-author of *How Psychology Applies to Everyday Life* (Greenwood Publishing).

CHARLES I. BROOKS is Professor and Chair of the Department of Psychology, King's College, Wilkes-Barre, Pennsylvania. He received his bachelor's degree in psychology from Duke University, his master's in psychology from Wake Forest University, and his doctorate in experimental psychology from Syracuse University. He has taught at King's College since 1975 and was designated a distinguished service professor in 1993. He has authored numerous scholarly publications in psychology and is co-author of *How Psychology Applies to Everyday Life* (Greenwood Publishing).

Subtle suicide : our silent epidemic of ambivalence about living / Michael A. Church and Charles I. Brooks.

DATE DUE

DEMCO, INC. 38-2931